White

Red

SERENA, FOOD & STORIES

FEEDING FRIENDS EVERY HOUR OF THE DAY

SERENA BASS

PHOTOGRAPHY BY DAVID LOFTUS AND ANDRA NELKI

ILLUSTRATIONS BY DAVID CROLAND

FOOD STYLING BY SUSIE THEODOROU

STEWART, TABORI & CHANG

FOOD

STORIES

FOR

JOE AND TINA

SAM AND KATHRYN

RECIPE FOR SUCCESS

1 A lot of people would like to glance at a page and absorb the idea of a recipe in a few seconds. If a dish sounds interesting—something you would like to try—I am begging you to take a moment and read the whole recipe through from start to finish. Try to imagine the cooking steps as you go and notice the order of ingredients used. Many times I've been halfway through a recipe, and have suddenly noticed . . . hmm, half the sugar goes in AFTER the apples . . . who knew? Well, you'll know if you give yourself the gift of one or two minutes' reading. Reading, and tasting at every stage, will help you arrive at perfection.

2 There are a few hard-to-find ingredients in the recipes, and the resources for them are listed on page 211. In this day of online shopping it's very easy to build your store of interesting condiments or spices and with it your reputation as a dedicated cook. You can order anything you might need ahead of time and have the best food the world has to offer at your fingertips.

3 Keep on cooking. Build up your culinary muscles. Simmer stocks, whisk mayonnaise, mince garlic, preserve some lemons, ice a cake, pound rouille, grill crostini, boil marmalade, shred Brussels sprouts, and braise beef. Keep a fridge full of strong mustard and have a good time.

HEARTFELT THANKS TO ALL THE LOVELY PEOPLE WHO HELPED MAKE THIS BOOK A REALITY
It starts with my great friend Gillian Duffy, the food editor of *New York* magazine who luckily decided to do a story about me entertaining guests in my country house. Clever Sandy Gilbert, my long-suffering editor, saw the article and, way before anyone else, envisioned a book. Diane Ormrod appropriated my scribbles and transformed them into a book proposal. Via Dorothy Hamilton, I found Alice Martell, über agent extraordinaire, who took me under her thoroughbred wing. My dearest friend Evie Righter with the patience and disposition of a summer day (including the thunder) showed me how to move forward in an organized manner; thanks to Jane Stouffer, who is so funny and smart, and also to Jane Kayantas (queen of the MAC laptop) and supremely benevolent aide; Eduard Riddle master of all the flowers and with Jill Levine keeper of the home fires. Thank you dear Carmen for your example, and Zara Mirza my Zanax in human form. Mauro Asitimbay who tested so many recipes and Kim Moss who created recipes, and always cared. Jonathan Adler whose stylish teapot, bowls, and plates grace many photographs and Simon Doonan who egged me on initially; and to Theo.

Thanks to my mentor and champion, Brooke Hayward, and to dear Andy Harris, for introducing me to David Loftus (a new friend for eternity) who with quiet and brilliant genius took most of the luscious photographs. Working with him and Susie Theodorou (the divine food stylist direct from Mount Olympus) we laughed and made beauty for five days straight even though the comma became an exclamation mark. My darling sister Andra Nelki, who also took amazing, witty photographs; we stood in the rain, the dark, and the middle of the road. We dealt with boisterous dogs, a collapsing tripod, and a burnt carpet. And love and kisses to the other sisters Beth and Gaynor who listened to endless variations of stories read over the phone to London ("No, you HAVEN'T heard this one.") John Barrett and Parvin Klein together perform happy miracles. My visionary friends, Sam Shahid and Frederico Farina, who worked so passionately and together designed a stunning book, I adore you both. Kindred spirit, Katie Sparks—a beautiful, talented cook and inspirational friend. And dearest— Kathy Rosenzweig, Laura Kirar, Richard Frazier, Richard Lambertson, John Truex, Linda and Brian Gracie, Page Dickey, Bosco Schell, Scott and Harriet Kaufman, Richard Turley, Robert Bergman, Ann and Clinton Howell, Lisa Hall, Linda Fargo, Michael Roberts, and the rock in my life, Scott Henry. Never were there any better, or kinder and more encouraging friends.

And above all, my beloved boys; thanks to my son Joe Shaffer for his inexhaustible kindness and wise council, and my darling daughter-in-law Tina; they both soothed and cheered me on throughout the whole process; and Sam Shaffer (with his lovely Kathryn) who evolved from son to business partner to my indispensable right hand and every day creates the fun in my life. *And the very final thanks to Ruby who sticks by me always—not that she has a choice.*

My mother died when I was eight. This fact has defined my life so entirely that it has even become the first line of my first book.

What happened *three weeks later* was that my father, an old but still frisky man, married a woman called Ann. Daddy was from the north of England, and was passionate for (to me) alarming things like blood sausage, head cheese, pig's feet, and tripe . . . and also very nice things like Yorkshire pudding and custard tarts. Ann herself had a predilection for chopped liver. You can only imagine the ordeal it was for me to enter my stepmother's kitchen in search of food. I would open the fridge, and since she was a dutiful wife, I would find trembling, offal-filled jellies, and sometimes little hooves on a plate. Once while trying to discover something I could eat, I took a spoonful of chocolate mousse, but unfortunately, it was the chopped liver.

Anyway, I became a cheese omelet and/or baked beans on toast kind of a girl, with an occasional treat of fried tomatoes and bacon on fried bread. I might even choose this combination for my last meal on earth if I was scheduled to die at dawn. No sweetbreads or lobster for me—I'm a very cheap date.

I wasn't allowed to cook or even help in the kitchen with Ann. I was somewhat intrigued by the process of turning raw ingredients into dinner on the table, but usually more repelled by the sights and viscous smells that are the hallmarks of my childhood memories of food.

I LOVED school food. I went to boarding school and absolutely couldn't understand the other girls complaining so bitterly at mealtime. As far as I was concerned, the shepherd's pie was utterly delicious, the cauliflower cheese sublime, and the spotted dick (a steamed pudding full of dark raisins) totally top-notch. We had a sweets (candy) handout once a week, so that was also something to look forward to.

I was born Serena Millington and our house mistress's name was Middleton. To my wicked friends, the similarity of form could not be ignored. I perfected her signature and traded forged "get out of games" notes for chocolate bars and lemon sherbets (my favorites). This ruse was so popular that I became a little porky and, realizing this, moved on to swapping notes for postage stamps—which, I'm sorry to say, I would subsequently sell back to other pupils. A very dubious first business, but 100 percent profit margin, unless you count the points scored against you by God.

My three older sisters were beautiful, funny, loving, and sadly absent (having been banished after the remarriage). I'd visit them in London during my school holidays. *I hung around with them and their boyfriends, got smuggled into pubs, and—disguised with lipstick that was supposed to make a twelve-year-old look eighteen—went to terrifying Luis Buñuel films and became nervous of dwarves and nuns.* My sisters would have people over for dinner all the time, but still I didn't cook, as firstly, I didn't have the foggiest idea of how to help, and secondly, they said I was on holiday and I should RELAX. But I started watching and thinking.

They had rented a basement apartment with a bathtub in the kitchen and we used a big board resting on top of the bath as a kitchen table. That might sound quite Dickensian, but we thought it fun. The landlord didn't know we thought it fun and only charged two pounds a week. I was never happier than sitting on a stool in a corner of that kitchen, listening to my sisters and their friends recount risqué stories of life in London; everyone shouting with laughter, Chianti flowing like Chianti, and Miles Davis seeping out of a transistor radio. The clever sister, Andra, already had a serious boyfriend whose words we hung upon. The sophisticated sister, Gaynor, had a dubious, older Italian boyfriend whose words we usually couldn't understand, and the sexy sister, Beth, well, she enjoyed a devoted, changeable group that didn't talk much at all. We knew one of them was coming round when she saucily slipped a red sock over the naked light bulb in the living room for atmosphere. It probably made the place look like a Dutch brothel, but we all thought it terribly exotic. The sock only caught fire once.

Whether the men in their lives talked or not, they all ate, and hardly a night went by without a huge bowl of pasta being produced around nine o'clock. Early on in the month it was full of chicken, mid-month it was canned tuna, and toward the end of the month clever things would be done with herbs. It was at one of these dinners, when I was about thirteen, that I suddenly realized the nature of a successful evening with friends. There was no formality—most people had been there so often before, they knew where everything was, especially the corkscrew and the ashtrays. The talk was seamless, coats were hung up, the table was laid, pots stirred, bottles opened, flowers stuffed into vases, all in a gorgeously warm recreation of the home that had slipped away from me years before. I felt as though I belonged in the middle of all of these attractive, witty people and was determined to find a way to make this feeling become a large part of my life.

I left school when I was sixteen and moved to London to go to college. I was met at Victoria Station by Beth and her current boyfriend (my future husband . . . the plot thickens). We three went out to movies and dinner together as, in a fit of kindness, they didn't want me to be left alone at home. This is relevant due to what happened next. Beth went off modeling somewhere abroad, and the future husband and I continued to go out as per usual. Beth was gone for QUITE A WHILE.

One night, after going to Ronnie Scott's Jazz Club in London's Soho, we came back very late to my house. He said, "I'm starving, would you make me some scrambled eggs?" Well, I was not about to admit that I had never cooked at all before, so I just did what I had seen my sisters do. The result elicited these fatal words: *These are the best eggs I've ever eaten. Why don't we have a dinner party?* Strangely, this didn't bother me. A dinner party was fun, everyone had a good time, and nothing was a problem.

He bought me Elizabeth David's *French Provincial Cooking* and I read the book cover to cover as some people do with the Bible. I read, learned, and inwardly digested every evocative word. I walked the gaudy, herb-scented markets of Provence, I prodded the fattened geese of Perigord, I tasted the fresh sweet butter of Normandy, and I stepped into another world.

Five days after the egg incident, we had six of his friends over for dinner. I made pâté de campagne, my finger tracing the words on the page. The pheasants I bought had recently been flapping around a Scottish moor, and I picked out as much buckshot as I could find, making a mental note to warn the guests. Then I flambéed the birds with Armagnac and braised them with Cox's Orange Pippin apples. For pudding (dessert)—since we only considered the condition of our hearts on Valentine's Day—I made crème brûlée and pears poached in wine served with clotted cream. Who knows how I made all this? I chatted away while I cooked, and there was no frowning; it was like ballroom dancing without staring at your feet, and I felt as though I'd come home. Cooking was easy, and since at sixteen I looked about twelve, when all this fancy food was delivered to the table, it produced such cries of astonishment and delight (not to mention the praise) that I determined to cook a great deal in the future. And so I did.

Caramelized Tomatoes

Sausage

Bacon

Fried Eggs

Fried Bread

Orange Marmalade

ENGLISH BREAKFAST AND THE FEAR OF FRYING When I was eighteen, I started going to Cape Town regularly for Christmas with the future husband. His English mother lived in a house lifted straight out of a luxurious London suburb, with silk rugs, oil paintings, hard-covered books, and comfortable beds. Every morning we'd wake to a strange combination: the smell of bacon wafting under our door and intense heat radiating through the window. It was England and yet . . . it was Africa. We'd put on our swimsuits, throw suntan lotion, hats, and books in a bag, and head downstairs for breakfast before hitting the beach. In the dining room were silver dishes stacked with crisp bacon, big, fat, pork and sage sausages, neat rows of fried bread triangles, caramelized tomatoes, and lovely fried eggs with brown lacy edges. This Anglican feast was set on a table in front of a large window, outside of which a draped curtain of shocking pink bougainvillea framed the sapphire Indian Ocean.

Having made complete pigs of ourselves, we'd be ready to stagger down to the beach, but warm toast would appear in silver toast racks plus a little crystal pot of homemade marmalade that was so awfully good, it demanded to be eaten straight with a spoon until it was all gone.

Charlie the cook was moderately good about sharing his recipes, mainly by example, as he didn't read or write or, in fact, speak much at all. However, the information on the marmalade wasn't to be had, and I was resigned to eating as much of it as I could while I was there and then waiting fifty weeks till I would go back. Pleas for a little extra to take home to England were roundly ignored.

(Hooray—its equal has been discovered. See the recipe on page 19.)

If you make any or all of this memorable meal, it's worth your while to get exceptional bacon and sausage. My absolutely favorite bacon is the cob-smoked breakfast bacon from Harrington's in Vermont. I just can't adequately relay the sweet, salty smokiness, or the perfect balance of fat to lean—all I can say is if people ask for two slices, give them four so they won't steal yours or force you to get up and make some more. I prefer to cook bacon in the oven—less mess and less attention. It also frees up the stovetop for making the Caramelized Tomatoes, and Fried Eggs (recipes follow).

CARAMELIZED TOMATOES

The best tomatoes for breakfast are tomatoes on the vine. If you were lucky and had a huge country estate and staff to match, the head gardener's third assistant would bring a wicker basket of tomatoes like these, from the greenhouse to the cook first thing in the morning. Yes, well . . . back in the supermarket, one way to tell if the tomatoes are going to have any flavor is to smell them. You want a sunny, earthy scent, with a hint of green citrus (a bit like geraniums) that is evident in locally grown summer tomatoes, but it is still possible to find in winter. Summer, winter, or whenever, keep them out of the fridge or their flavor will disappear like lightning.

1 medium vine-ripened tomato per person, cut in half horizontally

Maldon salt (see Resources, page 211) or kosher salt to taste

Freshly ground black pepper to taste

1 tablespoon unsalted butter

1 teaspoon vegetable oil

Put the tomatoes cut-side down on paper towels for a minute to drain some of their juices, then turn them over and sprinkle well with salt and pepper. Melt the butter with the oil in a skillet over low heat. Add the tomatoes cut side down and raise the heat to medium. Cook for 5 minutes, then flip the tomatoes and cook for 5 more minutes. Flip them once more and cook for another 5 minutes, or until they're nicely caramelized and meltingly soft all the way through.

SAUSAGE

The Cumberland sausages from Myers of Keswick, in Manhattan's Greenwich Village, are spectacular. Peter Myers still makes them himself every day from a recipe his grandfather was given in 1907. These particular sausages are juicy but very low in fat, and tangy with sage and white pepper. (Fortunately for non-New Yorkers, they may be ordered directly and sent by FedEx overnight.) (see Resources, page 211)

1 to 2 Cumberland sausages per person

Position a rack in the top third of the oven and preheat to 350°F.

Put the sausages on a baking sheet two inches apart and don't prick them yet. Place in the oven. Peter Myers says after 10 minutes prick them three times with a small, sharp knife to release some of their juices. Then cook for another 10 minutes (total cooking time is 20 minutes). However, the best way to tell whether they're done is with your own eye— if they're golden brown and shiny, they're good and ready.

BACON

2 to 4 slices Harrington bacon (see Resources, page 211) per person

Position a rack in the middle of the oven and preheat to 350°F.

Lay the bacon slices in rows on a baking sheet. Place in the oven for 15 to 20 minutes, or until the bacon is cooked the way you like it. Transfer the bacon to a platter lined with paper towels and keep warm until serving time.

FRIED EGGS

The main reason to seek out organic, newly laid eggs is their fresh flavor. When you're used to eggs from what my Aunt Jessica used to call "run-around chickens," any other kind seem pale by comparison. Eggs bought in a supermarket could have been laid weeks earlier, and sometimes the white is so broken down that it runs into a flat puddle when cracked into the pan. Unless you have a friend with a chicken hobby, or a farm in the country, farmers' markets are the best source of fresh eggs. Even if you don't see any for sale, a little questioning might result in the sealing of a weekly deal for a dozen speckled eggs that will virtually stand up and salute you on the plate and could be brought into town just for you. The crispy, frilly edge (my ideal) on a fried egg will only develop during the first few seconds in the pan if the oil is very hot. I use vegetable oil and probably twice as much salt and pepper as you might imagine.

3 tablespoons vegetable oil

1 to 2 free-range eggs per person

Kosher salt to taste

Freshly ground black pepper to taste

First, put on an apron and make sure everything else is ready and on the table. I prefer to cook one egg at a time so the fat stays really hot. Pour the oil into a small nonstick pan over medium heat and warm the oil to shimmering. Crack in an egg—its perimeter will bubble wildly and shortly become brown and crisp. Generously sprinkle on salt and pepper. Let the egg fry away for a minute, then flip it over and cook the top for 30 seconds, or if you doubt your flipability skills, spoon the fat over the egg until the white is firm and the yolk cooked the way you like it. [In my catering kitchen the guys always break the yolk and cook it through *(and through)*, sandwiching the eggs in a soft roll with blazingly hot Scotch bonnet sauce, so there's no accounting for taste.] If you do turn the

egg over, turn it back—right side up—onto a paper towel to drain for a moment. Serve on a warm plate with any or all of the other English things I'm extolling.

FRIED BREAD

Now, *fried bread just sounds bad*. In reality, it's better for you than a doughnut because it's exactly the same thing but flat and without all the sugar. Look for a nice sturdy white bread made with just flour, yeast, and salt—no additives, no preservatives, and no sugar.

White country bread, sliced at least $^1/_2$-inch thick, 1 slice per person

1 to 2 tablespoons vegetable oil

1 teaspoon bacon fat (optional)

Kosher salt to taste

Cut the crusts off the bread. Heat the oil (with the bacon fat, if you fancy) over medium heat in a skillet. Add the bread slices and fry about 1 minute on both sides, to a golden brown, then sprinkle lightly with salt and serve very hot.

RUTH CAMPBELL'S MARMALADE

My marmalade fetish is not just a personal thing. With a little prodding, virtually anyone with a teaspoon of English blood in them will admit to the same predilection. You can buy marmalade everywhere, but there is something particularly satisfying about making it yourself, exactly the way you prefer it. I happen to like chunky bits of peel suspended in a fairly tart, slightly runny jelly.

I came upon this wonderful marmalade while staying on Shelter Island for the weekend with my friend Nell Campbell. She's Australian, hugely stylish, and a star raconteur/cook/mother/actor/dancer who tends to carry on nimble conversations while stretching gracefully toward her foot, which (for the stretching purpose) she might lodge on the mantel of a fireplace or the hood of an SUV.

We sat together at the breakfast table that particular Sunday morning, looking out over Long Island Sound. It was a toast-driven breakfast—homemade bread with salted butter (very antipodean) and Marmite (ditto), which I love, but a little goes a long way. I wanted something sweet and said so. Nell jumped up, reached into a cupboard, and, putting a jar on the table, said in her best Australian, "Try Mummy's marmalade, darling." I did and it was spectacular.

ORANGE MARMALADE
Makes 8 cups

I buy "sour" (Seville) oranges at my local Spanish bodega. They're available all year round and are much cheaper than in a fancy gourmet food shop; just look for fruit with a bright orange skin, as it can be green or a murky yellow.

1 1/2   pounds whole Seville oranges, washed and quartered

1   whole lemon, washed and quartered

7   cups sugar

Using a paring knife, remove the seeds and central white membrane from the orange and lemon quarters. Put the seeds and membrane into a small saucepan with 1 cup water, cover, and boil for 30 minutes to produce pectin. During this time, slice the peel and attached fruit once or twice down the middle of each section, then across into $1/4$-inch strips or thinner if you prefer. Put the peel in a large saucepan with 6 cups water. Boil until the fruit is translucent, about 40 minutes. Keep an eye on the small saucepan and strain the pectin—pressing down on the solids—into the large saucepan when it's ready.

Add the sugar and stir to melt. Bring the mixture back to a boil, and stir occasionally for 30 minutes. Begin testing by spooning a little marmalade onto a cold saucer, then put in the freezer for at least 5 minutes. When you take it out, the marmalade should be set. (While testing, turn the heat to low.) If it hasn't set, continue to boil and test again every 5 minutes.

Immediately spoon into sterilized glass jars (see Note). Screw the lids on firmly and the next day, tighten the lids again. You can store the marmalade at room temperature but keep it in the fridge once opened. The unopened jars of marmalade should be good for up to a year.

Note: To sterilize, place the jars and lids in a large saucepan and cover with water; bring to a boil, and boil for 20 minutes, topping up with more boiling water as needed. Carefully remove the jars and lids with tongs, drain and air-dry.

RELAX . . . YOU'RE AMONG FRIENDS

I know the very word "relax" might make you get terribly anxious, imagining a bunch of cheery friends full of great expectations arriving at your door before you've had your second cup of coffee. But with a little planning and some things done the night before, you can organize your life so everything will be ready with time to spare. When people arrive for lunch, they are usually still full from breakfast. When they arrive at my house for brunch, they're often STARVING and hardly have time for a kiss before diving headfirst into any food I've got waiting (those are my friends, anyway).

Since brunch demands quite a lot of interaction with the food—what with spreading cream cheese on bagels, squeezing lemon on smoked salmon, and pouring maple syrup on pancakes—I like to make sure everyone has a seat. I've found that if people can sit around the table, they'll eat. If they can only stand because you don't have enough chairs, they'll just drink and maybe chew on a bagel. If you need to expand into other areas of the house or apartment, put more of everything—glasses, carafes of orange juice, coffee in thermal pourers, mugs, spoons, milk, and sugar—on another table (maybe in the living room) so once people settle there, they don't have to keep getting up and down for refills.

THE NIGHT BEFORE

Luckily, almost everything can be set out before your guests arrive so there won't be any last-minute scramble. I lay the table the night before, arranging the empty baskets and platters and, if I'm in the mood, rolling the knives and forks in napkins. (If not, I just put them in a basket.) Vodka goes in the freezer and Asti Spumanti (absolutely the best thing with fruit purees—two cups of fruit pureed with $1/3$ to $1/2$ cup sugar—for making Bellinis) in the fridge, and I might even get a head start on some of the frittata fillings, like taking the sweet corn off the cob. The butter and cream cheese go in their dishes so they're ready to be put on the table the next morning, and, if not already arranged, I put flowers in vases.

IN THE MORNING

You can either make the muffins first thing so they cool down a bit, or you can take them out of the oven as your friends are arriving and they'll eat them right out of the pan with moans of bliss and possible minor burns.

Split the bagels nearly in half yourself and put a toaster on the table for the toasted bagel lovers. You might need an extension cord; if so, don't forget to tape the cord to the floor so no one takes a header over it. Put out a couple of WOODEN skewers for removing a "stuck-in-the-toaster" bagel, or you might add electrocution to all the excitement as guests poke around trying to get bagels out with the nearest metal knife.

I prefer to have cream cheese cool rather than cold; it's easier to spread and actually tastes better too, so if you agree, take it and the butter out of the fridge an hour beforehand. Separate each slice of smoked salmon and arrange it in little wavy billows so it can easily be picked up with a fork. I love those cans of real maple syrup with a picture of a cabin in the woods, but they always dribble horribly, so if I'm serving pancakes I usually decant the syrup into a "good pouring" little glass pitcher, which can go into the microwave to warm the syrup up a bit. A glass pitcher is better than ceramic so you can check from a distance if your guests have enough left. If you want to be rustically stylish, empty the maple syrup can and use it as a vase.

ORANGE JUICE

When you buy freshly squeezed orange juice, do try some before everyone arrives, as it can be amazingly good or very disappointing. If it's not as sweet as you had expected, add some sugar—you're only substituting for missing fructose. A little sugar goes a long way; just make sure it's totally dissolved and not sitting in a telltale layer at the bottom of the carafe. Don't be tempted to add honey or brown sugar (hoping to be more healthful) as it will throw the flavor off completely.

EUROPEAN PANCAKES
Makes 6 to 8 medium pancakes

Most people have a favorite pancake recipe, so I've avoided giving you yet another common or garden one. INSTEAD, I've gone

Germanic and developed something more in the direction of an apple pancake. These pancakes are big, delicate, tender, and slim (as opposed to fat or thin) and are rolled with a filling of blackberries warmed with sugar, lemon, and vanilla. You could also try them with blueberries or applesauce or cherry preserves—in fact, experiment away—I'm positive you could do no wrong.

2 cups sour cream

4 extra-large eggs

3/4 teaspoon kosher salt

1 teaspoon baking soda

3 tablespoons sugar

3/4 cup Heckers or King Arthur all-purpose flour

Unsalted butter for the pan

Blackberry Compote (recipe follows)

Confectioners', or superfine sugar for dusting

Lemon wedges for serving

Dump the sour cream, eggs, salt, baking soda, sugar, and flour in a deep bowl, and whisk to blend well. Set a 9- to 10-inch square non-stick griddle over low heat and leave it for 3 minutes to warm through thoroughly, then very lightly brush the surface with butter. Turn the heat to medium and, to make 1 large pancake, using a 1/3 cup measure, pour the batter onto the pan. When bubbles start to form and then pop, slip a big spatula underneath and turn the pancake over with a fluid movement. (Bear in mind that this is a floppy pancake; don't leave it hanging off the spatula as it will tear.) Cook another minute, then shake the pancake to loosen it, and tip it over onto a plate. Spoon a little Blackberry Compote over the surface of the pancake, then loosely roll it up and dust with confectioners' or superfine sugar. These are perfectly wonderful with just lemon and sugar if you don't feel much like making the compote. Gently insist everyone squeezes lemon over their pancakes; you'll discover it will make a delicious difference.

BLACKBERRY COMPOTE
Makes 2 1/4 cups

Like any compote, this is better the next day when the berries have soaked up some of their juice. If refrigerated overnight, warm the compote before using it in the pancakes. Try spooning any extra compote over vanilla ice cream or lemon sherbet.

18 ounces fresh blackberries

6 tablespoons sugar (or more if the blackberries are very tart)

Zest of 1 lemon

1 1/2 teaspoons pure vanilla extract

Put the blackberries, sugar, and lemon zest in a small, heavy saucepan over low heat. Cook for about 5 minutes, stirring occasionally as the juices start to run. Remove from the heat, stir in the vanilla, and set aside to cool.

FRITTATAS

I love a frittata. It can be wildly creative or simple and pure, and gives an indication of home cooking among a sea of store-bought bagels. Plus, frittatas can sit around once made, waiting for people to help themselves, unlike scrambled eggs, which have about a three minute optimum shelf life. One type of frittata is PERFECTLY FINE, but while you're at it, two or even three types are quite impressive and not that much more work—just a bit more shopping and chopping. I like the idea of cooking a frittata in the sort of pan that an Italian grandmother would probably have used: some seven-pound cast-iron skillet, never washed, just scoured with sea salt and smooth as a baby's bottom, but since non-stick pans exist . . . those are the pans for me.

GENERAL FRITTATA GUIDELINES

Get your pan uniformly hot (over a low heat to warm the sides as well as the base) before adding the filling, and have a spatula nearby. Remember, if you're adding the eggs to a filling that's already hot in the pan, the eggs will firm up quite fast. Using the spatula, keep pulling the edge of the eggs to the middle; tip and shake the pan so the uncooked egg runs onto the hot metal.

When there is still a little uncooked egg left on top, put the frittata in the pan into the oven to finish cooking.

If you're not sure whether the frittata is ready, hold the handle of the pan with a heavy oven mitt and tip the pan at an angle for about five seconds. If lots of uncooked egg runs out from the middle, it will need another couple of minutes; if just a little runs out, you can remove it from the oven and the frittata will finish cooking in its own heat.

** A word of caution—you know the handle of the frittata pan is hot, but not everyone wandering around the kitchen may be so aware. Wrap a thick kitchen towel around the handle when it comes out of the oven to avoid accidents.

Seasoning in layers is something a lot of people forget to do, but it's the key to success in all composed dishes. In any frittata, season the eggs, then season the filling. Since cheese is often one of the fillings, try a bit before you add it. It may be very salty like feta or some Parmesans, or mild like mozzarella—this knowledge will help you season astutely. A pinch of kosher salt, some freshly ground black pepper, and fresh herbs on top just before serving (whether hot or at room temperature) will add another layer of flavor.

If the frittata is destined for room temperature, slide it onto a plate and tuck a strip of paper towel around its perimeter to mop up any escaping juices until serving time. Then set it on a bed of roughly chopped watercress or arugula that has been lightly tossed with a little sharp vinaigrette. A frittata is a rich thing and needs a bit of sparky salad to complement it. If you are serving the frittata warm, then just put out a bowl of dressed salad for people to take as they like.

SHRIMP, CHORIZO, AND MANCHEGO FRITTATA

Serves 6 (see photograph, page 25)

One weekend I had friends staying with me from Barcelona and, inspired by them, rather bravely made a frittata that would have been more at home in the shadow of Gaudí's Casa Milà than in the Connecticut woods. No matter, they approved. Later in the day as the sun set, we sat on the deck with a bottle of fine Rioja, and ate black olives with the left-over frittata, cut in little squares, then dipped into a saucer of aged balsamic. The woods felt rather more international than usual.

10 extra-large eggs

1 teaspoon kosher salt

1 teaspoon freshly ground black pepper

2 tablespoons fruity olive oil

1 medium yellow onion, chopped medium

2 garlic cloves, chopped

1/2 pound chorizo sausage, chopped medium

1/4 pound raw shrimp, peeled and deveined, chopped medium

3 ounces Manchego cheese, grated

Position a rack in the middle of the oven and preheat to 350°F.

In a large bowl, whisk the eggs with the salt and pepper and set aside. Place a 9-inch nonstick sauté pan over medium heat, add the oil, onion, and garlic, and cook for 3 minutes; turn up the heat, add the chorizo, and cook until the onions caramelize a little, about 5 minutes. Add the shrimp and cook for 2 minutes, stirring occasionally, to evaporate any water they exude, then turn down the heat and add the eggs. Using a heatproof spatula, pull the edges of the frittata to the middle a few times, tipping the pan to distribute the egg. Cook for about 4 minutes, scatter on the Manchego, and finish in the oven for 6 minutes, or until the eggs are delicately set. (Don't forget to wrap the handle of the pan with a towel when it comes out of the oven.) Let the frittata sit for a minute; then, if you're serving it immediately, with the help of a spatula slide it onto a warm plate. If it's destined for room temperature, slide it onto a plate and set it aside until you need it. Serve it on watercress or arugula dressed with a little vinaigrette, heavy on the mustard.

NEW POTATO, JALAPEÑO, AND MINT FRITTATA

Serves 6

This is an interesting frittata for vegetarians. It has a wonderfully complex bunch of flavors, as the potatoes, cooked in this way, become almost sweet and vie for supremacy over the spicy jalapeño and the herbal mint.

10 extra-large eggs

2 teaspoons kosher salt, divided

1/2 teaspoon freshly ground black pepper

4 tablespoons (1/2 stick) unsalted butter

1 medium yellow onion, diced medium

1/2 pound small new potatoes (red or white), sliced very thin

1 seeded jalapeño (depending on your taste and the taste of the jalapeño)

2 tablespoons minced fresh mint leaves (about 12 leaves)

Position a rack in the middle of the oven and preheat to 350°F.

In a large bowl whisk the eggs with 1 teaspoon of the salt and the pepper and set aside. Melt the butter in a 9-inch nonstick sauté pan over medium heat; add the onions and sauté for 3 minutes. Add the potatoes and the remaining teaspoon of salt and cook, turning occasionally, for 10 minutes, then add the jalapeño and cook for a minute, or until the potatoes are cooked through. Pour the eggs into the pan, scatter on the mint; then shake the pan so the egg settles under the potatoes. Using a heatproof spatula, start pulling the edges of the frittata to the middle and keep tipping the pan to distribute the egg. Cook for about 4 minutes, shake the pan a couple of times to level the eggs, and then put the pan in the oven for about 6 minutes, or until the eggs are delicately set. (Don't forget to wrap the handle of the pan with a towel when it comes out of the oven.) Let the frittata sit for a minute, then, if you're serving it immediately, with the help of a spatula slide it onto a warm plate. If it's destined for room temperature, just put it on a plate and set aside until you need it. Serve on some baby lettuce dressed with a lemony vinaigrette.

FRESH SWEET CORN, SUN-DRIED TOMATO, AND BASIL FRITTATA
Serves 6

Sun-dried tomatoes and sweet corn work together perfectly in every way—the color, texture, and taste can hardly be improved. It's a summer day on a plate.

10 extra-large eggs

1/3 cup oil-packed sun-dried tomatoes, drained and chopped medium

2 garlic cloves, crushed

1 1/4 teaspoons kosher salt

3/4 teaspoon freshly ground black pepper

3 ears sweet corn (to make 2 cups of kernels)

2 tablespoons unsalted butter

2 tablespoons chopped fresh basil leaves

Position a rack in the middle of the oven and preheat to 350°F.

If you have time the night before, whisk the eggs in a large bowl and stir in the sun-dried tomatoes, garlic, 1 teaspoon of the salt, and 1/2 teaspoon of the pepper; leave covered in the fridge. The tomatoes will plump up, and the flavors will have a chance to expand. If you like, you can also cook the corn the night before. In a small saucepan, bring a cup of lightly salted water to a boil. Add the sweet corn and cook, stirring, until still a little crunchy, 5 to 7 minutes. Drain well and toss with the remaining 1/4 teaspoon of salt, and pepper. Cover and refrigerate.

Melt the butter in a 9-inch nonstick sauté pan over medium-high heat; when it starts to foam, add the corn (if it's cold from the fridge, warm it well), the egg mixture, and the basil. Using a heatproof spatula, pull the edges of the frittata to the middle a few times, tipping the pan to distribute the egg. Cook for about 4 minutes and finish in the oven for 6 minutes, or until the eggs are delicately set. (Don't forget to wrap the handle of the pan with a towel when it comes out of the oven so no one gets a hand-brand by mistake.) Let the frittata sit for a minute, then, with the help of a spatula, slide it onto a warm plate, or if it's destined for room temperature, just put it on a plate and set it aside until you need it. Serve on arugula tossed with balsamic vinaigrette.

OTHER TRIED-AND-TRUE FRITTATA COMBINATIONS

1 Prosciutto di Parma, Smoked Mozzarella, Fresh Thyme
2 Grilled Portobello Mushrooms, Rosemary, Pine Nuts
3 Virginia Ham, Green Peas, Parsley
4 Black Beans, Salsa, Pepper Jack Cheese
5 Smoked Fish (Trout, Salmon, Haddock, or Sturgeon), Chives
6 Spinach and Feta sprinkled with Olive Oil-Fried Breadcrumbs

MUFFINS

My catering company is now situated on West Thirteenth Street in the meatpacking district of Manhattan. We use muffins as the bribe of choice to get the sanitation men to move our extra garbage, bloody butchers to move their carnage, and the super next door to hose down our sidewalk when we can't be bothered. No one can resist these muffins and, once tasted, a powerful addiction springs up.

The plum and almond muffins are a comfort for people who want to appear healthy, as a lovely slice of plum rests on the top; the carrot and date are *a little sticky and unnaturally tender*; and the mocha oatmeal (full of walnuts, espresso, and chocolate chips) are considered a bit of a walk on the wild side. The carrot and the mocha ones are best when the batter is made the day before. With the extra time, the carrot batter firms up and the oatmeal in the mocha batter expands. To make your life easier, the plum one is also fine with the batter made the day before.

Measure the dry ingredients before the wet so you don't have to wash the measuring cups. I like to spoon the batter straight into well-greased muffin tins and then store overnight in the refrigerator. In the morning, all you have to do is scatter on the toppings and put the muffins into a preheated oven with no fuss and bother.

If you want a raspberry, peach, or apricot muffin you can use the plum and almond recipe, substituting the fruit of your choice.

CARROT AND DATE MUFFINS

Makes 12 muffins

THE DRY INGREDIENTS

1   cup plus 2 tablespoons Heckers or King Arthur all-purpose flour

$3/4$ teaspoon baking powder

$3/4$ teaspoon baking soda

$1/4$ teaspoon kosher salt

$3/4$ teaspoon cinnamon

THE WET INGREDIENTS

2   extra-large eggs

$1/2$ cup vegetable oil, plus some for greasing the muffin tin

$1/4$ cup molasses

$3/4$ cup sugar

1 $1/2$ cups firmly packed grated carrots

$1/3$ cup pitted dates, each cut into 6 pieces

6   dates, pitted and cut in half lengthwise, for decoration

Sugar for sprinkling on top

Position a rack in the top third of the oven and preheat to 350°F. Grease the muffin tin and set aside.

Sift the dry ingredients together into a wide, shallow bowl. In a deep bowl, whisk the eggs with the oil, molasses, and sugar; stir in the carrots and dates. Pour the wet ingredients over the dry and, with as few gentle strokes as possible, fold them together. I stop folding when there's still a little flour visible. Spoon into the muffin tin; lay a date half on top of each muffin, and sprinkle the tops with sugar. Bake for 20 to 25 minutes, or until the muffins are firm. After 5 minutes, remove from the tin and cool on a rack.

PLUM AND ALMOND MUFFINS

Makes 12 muffins

THE DRY INGREDIENTS

2   cups Heckers or King Arthur all-purpose flour

$3/4$ teaspoon baking powder

1   teaspoon baking soda

1   teaspoon kosher salt

$3/4$ cup sugar plus extra for sprinkling on top

THE WET INGREDIENTS

5   tablespoons vegetable oil, plus some for greasing the muffin tin

1   extra-large egg

$3/4$ teaspoon pure vanilla extract

$1/2$ teaspoon pure almond extract

1   cup buttermilk

1 $1/2$ cups plums (halved, pitted, and cut into rough $1/2$-inch cubes)

1   whole plum, pitted and cut into 12 wedges, for decoration

Position a rack in the top third of the oven and preheat to 350°F. Grease the muffin tin and set it aside.

Sift the dry ingredients into a wide, shallow bowl, which will make it easier to FOLD rather than stir everything together. Beat the wet ingredients in a deep bowl good for whisking without splashing. Pour the wet ingredients over the dry and, with as few gentle strokes as possible, fold them together. I stop folding when there's still a little flour visible; the batter will pick up moisture by association, and the muffins will be tender instead of rubbery. Spoon into the muffin tin, press a plum wedge down into each muffin, and sprinkle with sugar. Bake for 20 to 25 minutes or until the muffins are golden brown and firm to the touch. Allow to cool for 10 minutes, giving the juicy plums time to calm down, before removing the muffins from the tin.

MOCHA OATMEAL MUFFINS
Makes 16 muffins

One day, or rather night, I found myself trying to get a head start on the next day's catering jobs by making muffin batter at one A.M. Sometimes it seems we couldn't possibly be missing a single ingredient in the whole world in our kitchen, but of course, when I really needed it, the toasted wheat germ had gone AWOL. In a sleepy daze, I used oatmeal, deciding one carb was as good as another. Well, I liked this terrific recipe, by Margaret Fox from her cookbook, *Morning Food from Café Beaujolais*, even more than usual.

Nowadays we always use oatmeal, and the dusting of flakes looks reassuringly healthy scattered on the top of this rich, intensely flavored muffin.

If you don't need sixteen muffins, you can freeze half the batter for up to a month.

THE DRY INGREDIENTS

1/3   cup cocoa powder (see Resources, page 211)

1 1/2   cups Heckers or King Arthur all-purpose flour

1 1/4   cups Quaker 5-Minute Oatmeal, plus extra for the top

1   cup light brown sugar

1/2   teaspoon baking powder

1   teaspoon baking soda

1 1/4   teaspoons kosher salt

THE WET INGREDIENTS

3 extra-large eggs

12 tablespoons (1 1/2 sticks) melted unsalted butter, plus extra for greasing the muffin tins

1 cup buttermilk

1 tablespoon Medaglia d'Oro espresso powder, dissolved in 1/2 cup boiling water

1 teaspoon pure vanilla extract

1 cup chocolate chips

1 cup walnut halves

Sugar for sprinkling on top

Position a rack in the middle of the oven and preheat to 350°F. Grease the muffin tins and set them aside.

Sift the dry ingredients together into a wide, shallow bowl, then stir through the oatmeal. In a deep bowl, beat the eggs, and then add the melted butter, buttermilk, espresso, and vanilla. Pour the wet ingredients over the dry, scatter on the chocolate chips and walnuts, and fold everything together with as few gentle strokes as possible. Spoon into the muffin tins; sprinkle with oatmeal and then sugar. Bake for 20 to 25 minutes, or until the muffins are just firm. Allow to cool for 10 minutes before removing the muffins from the tin.

Note: The batter should be made the day before and you can even spoon it into the muffin tins so it's ready for the oven the next day.

BAGELS

I would rather have no bagels than bad bagels. Even buying them in New York City is no guarantee of excellence, so the challenge of locating a decent bagel in Minneapolis or Kansas City is something to consider. At the very least, buy your bagels on the morning of the brunch—don't put them in the fridge—and keep the oniony/garlicky/salty ones away from the others. If you can find a shop where they make bagels on-site, you could try becoming friends with the owner and have them make you mini-bagels or bagel sticks—they're much less clunky than the big ones.

THINGS TO THINK ABOUT CONCERNING FRUIT

Straight-sided glass bowls make it easier to get the fruit into the serving spoon without having to chase it all around a plate.

Scatter a few wedges of lime on tropical fruit like mangoes and papaya for your guests to squeeze if they like.

Unpeeled Bartlett pears, cored, sliced, and tossed with a splash of fresh lemon juice to prevent them turning brown, develop a delicious haunting perfume.

If you serve strawberries unhulled, don't forget to put out a little bowl for the green tops.

The most delectable way to serve grapefruit is to cut away the peel and white pith. Hold the naked grapefruit in your hand over a bowl, and with a short, sharp knife, remove each section of fruit from its membrane. Squeeze the remaining pulp with your hand to get out all the juice. Put the segments in individual little glasses with a small fork (which is easier than a spoon for spearing the fruit). When the fruit has been eaten, guests can drink any remaining juice.

TIP

If you are serving food outside, think about the danger of broken glass. Shards of glass in the grass can lurk around for years, and the minute you have a barefoot child, they just make a beeline to it. Even if my guests are all grown-ups of a sober mind, I am inclined to find the nicest possible plastic glasses and use them instead.

MISCELLANEOUS TIP

If you have a world-class memory, go right ahead and invite random friends that you drive up abreast of at the traffic light— "Having some people over, do come . . . love to see you . . . twelve o'clock on . . . byeee." By one o'clock on the day of the brunch, with at least six more people than expected and car doors still slamming, I usually bitterly regret my bonhomie and fantasize about putting my head out of the window and shouting, "Go away, this brunch is now closed to the public."

I like to make a follow-up call. It helps confirm who's coming and sends a signal that it's a real meal, at a real time. It informs the guests that whether they're there or not is a matter of some importance, and WILL BE NOTED.

DOGS

If dogs are visiting, have a couple of big chewy rawhide bones handy to keep them busy. If you don't have a dog of your own, set up a water bowl somewhere inside on a towel *(slobber can travel)* and another (if you have a fenced-in yard) in a shady place outside, before the guests arrive. You don't want to be forced to use your best crystal because you can't find anything else and poor Spot is on the point of collapse.

REMEMBER

Many more than you expected? Requisition help—people love to come to the aid of the party. Many fewer people? Don't fret—in fact, don't give it another thought. Go ahead and get cozy. In England we would always have pencil and paper on hand and play games, yes, even at one o'clock in the afternoon. The only thing that can dampen a gathering inexorably is your own anxiety, so relax. You won't be the weakest link and you are surrounded by friends.

DAZZLING FOOD

And I'm talking about culinary fireworks that dazzle. The kind of food that engenders remarks which you may never hear . . . *"We can't possibly miss brunch with Serena"* (my fantasy). *"She might make that chocolate French toast with salted apples!"* As self-help books keep reminding us, "No one is thinking about YOU," but they may very well be thinking about your food. Here are some extra-ordinarily memorable brunch possibilities.

BURRITOS
Serves 6 to 8

The trick here is to get a heavy, preferably cast-iron skillet really hot, so when you lay in the flour tortilla, it quickly blackens and burns in a few spots, imparting a smokiness which, when paired with creamy scrambled eggs and cool spicy salsa, can't be beat. If you're not using store-bought salsa, make the salsa an hour ahead, so the flavors have time to permeate. These burritos are quite filling—half of a big tortilla is usually enough for one person.

6 extra-large eggs, scrambled (see recipe, page 42)

4 large flour tortillas

1 cup of your favorite spicy salsa

Preheat the oven to warm. Keep the scrambled eggs warm. Heat a large skillet to very hot and lay in 1 flour tortilla. Wait about 10 seconds, and using metal tongs, turn the tortilla over and heat for another 5 to 10 seconds. There should be a few black marks the size of a nickel on the first side and a speckling on the second side. Lay the hot tortilla (lighter side up) on a cutting board and spoon on a quarter of the scrambled eggs in a horizontal line centered on the tortilla half nearest you. Top with salsa. Fold over the edge nearest you, then fold in the sides and roll up neatly into a cylinder. Repeat with the remaining tortillas. The burritos can be kept warm in the oven for up to 15 minutes, but are best eaten immediately. Serve each burrito cut diagonally across the middle.

CHEESE AND CHERRY BLINTZES
Makes 12 blintzes

If you have ever had a frozen cheese and cherry blintz, please clear your mind, and let's start over.

We first developed this recipe for a late-night cocktail party at the Russian Consulate in Manhattan (only a little nerve-racking offering these to real Russians who would know a fabulous blintz from a failed blintz). The party was held for a musical prodigy from Moscow, plus two hundred of his admirers and patrons of his particular art. We started with little yeasty blinis topped with caviar and smoked sturgeon, and in the last hour, passed the blintzes. We had finished them off backstage (as it were) and they were still warm from the oven when we brought them out. Despite the excellent blinis, an impartial observer would have thought no one at that party had eaten for a week. The poor waiters were mobbed and the chef was very smug as, when I had commented on the amount prepared, she'd said, "Trust me, it may not even be enough."

These blintzes are a little bigger than those served at the consulate. Being larger they looked a bit naked, so I've embellished them with almonds and sugar.

THE CRÊPES

- $1/2$ cup Heckers or King Arthur all-purpose flour
- 2 extra-large eggs
- $1/2$ cup whole milk
- $1/2$ teaspoon kosher salt
- $1/2$ teaspoon pure vanilla extract
- 4 tablespoons ($1/2$ stick) unsalted butter, melted (for the crêpe mixture, the pan, and for buttering the blintzes)
- $1/3$ cup sliced blanched almonds for sprinkling, toasted at 350°F for 8 minutes
- 1 tablespoon sugar for sprinkling

Put the flour in a small deep bowl, add the eggs and with a balloon whisk, vigorously beat together until smooth. Add 2 tablespoons of water and whisk to smooth, then add 2 more tablespoons of water, and whisk again, then add the milk, salt, and vanilla, and whisk until thoroughly smooth. Cover the bowl and set it aside for half an hour.

When you come to cook the crêpes, add 1 tablespoon of melted butter to the batter and whisk through. Set a 7- to 8-inch nonstick frying pan over medium heat; when it's hot, brush very lightly with the melted butter; pour in 3 tablespoons of batter and quickly tip the pan in all directions to make a neat round shape. Tip any excess batter back in the bowl and don't worry about the lip running to the edge of the pan, you will flip that area over first when you enclose the filling.

Cook for about 45 seconds, or until the crêpe is curling at the edges and a pale golden brown underneath. Lift with a spatula and lay, cooked side down, on a sheet pan. Repeat until all the batter is used up.

THE CHEESE AND CHERRY FILLING

- One 7 $1/2$-ounce package Friendship Farmers Cheese, at room temperature
- 4 ounces cream cheese, softened
- 3 tablespoons sugar
- $3/4$ teaspoon pure almond extract
- 2 extra-large egg yolks
- One 14 $1/2$-ounce can (OR bag of frozen) dark cherries

Beat together the farmer's cheese, cream cheese, sugar, almond extract, and the egg yolks until completely smooth, and set aside. Position a rack in the upper third of the oven and preheat to 400°F.

TO ASSEMBLE

Place 1 $1/2$ tablespoons of the filling in the middle of each crêpe. Put 3 cherries on top and fold the crêpe up like an envelope, then roll to close.

Repeat with the remaining crêpes. Turn the blintzes in the melted butter and arrange them $1/2$ inch apart in rows in an ovenproof dish. Put a little pile of toasted almonds on each blintz and sprinkle with $1/4$ teaspoon sugar, then bake for 15 minutes. Serve warm.

CHOCOLATE FRENCH TOAST WITH SALTED APPLES
Serves 4

I specially love this recipe because you can get absolutely everything ready the day before. It's a bit like a warm chocolate croissant with fragrant apples sautéed in butter piled on top and sprinkled with Maldon (or kosher) salt to cut the richness. Maldon salt is preferable because the flakes are nice and big. Gala apples work very well—they're deliciously perfumed and hold their shape. They're also widely available, which is a huge plus as it's sometimes a bit irritating when you can't find the exact apple recommended in a recipe and you wonder what you're missing. Eliminating the sugar in the egg wash and using a plain white bread (as opposed to panettone or challah, which both contain sugar) allows for the inclusion of chocolate without the whole thing becoming deathly sweet. A loaf with a fairly even crumb is best, so the chocolate doesn't run out through any holes when it melts.

2 extra-large eggs

1/4 cup half-and-half

2 teaspoons pure vanilla extract

Four 1-inch-thick slices day-old bread

4 tablespoons chocolate chips (preferably Ghirardelli brand)

1 tablespoon unsalted butter

2 Gala apples at room temperature, quartered, cored, and cut into 12 wedges each

2 to 3 tablespoons vegetable oil

Kosher or Maldon salt to taste (see Resources, page 211)

Preheat the oven to 250°F. In a small bowl, whisk together the eggs, half-and-half, and vanilla. Pour the egg wash into a shallow dish that can hold the 4 slices of bread laid flat. Using a very sharp straight-bladed knife, trim the crusts off the bread, carefully cut a horizontal pocket in each bread slice big enough for the chocolate chips to spread out a bit, and not sit in a big lump. Fill each bread pocket with 1 tablespoon of chocolate chips and lay the bread slices in the egg wash. Let them soak for a minute, then turn them over and leave in the dish while you sauté the apples.

Heat a sauté pan over medium heat for 3 minutes, and then add the butter. When the butter has stopped sizzling, turn the heat to high, add the apples, and sauté until they are translucent and caramelized, about 5 minutes. *If the heat isn't high enough, the apples will sweat and steam and will never brown at the edges.* Transfer the apples to the oven in an ovenproof dish while you cook the French toast.

Heat the oil in a heavy sauté pan over medium high heat and add two slices of bread. Cook for 2 to 3 minutes per side to a crisp golden brown, adding more oil if needed. To serve, cut the slices diagonally and set one half on the other so the melted chocolate shows. Tip the apples on top and scatter with a little salt, preferably the Maldon.

SWEET POTATO LATKES WITH POACHED EGG, SMOKED SALMON, AND CHIVE CRÈME FRAÎCHE

Makes 10 latkes

1 pound sweet potatoes

1/2 pound Yukon Gold potatoes

1 medium yellow onion

2 extra-large eggs

1/3 cup all-purpose flour

1/2 teaspoon cayenne pepper (optional)

3/4 teaspoon freshly ground black pepper

1 to 2 tablespoons kosher salt, or to taste

Chive Crème Fraîche (recipe follows)

Vegetable oil for frying

1 ounce smoked salmon per person

Position a rack in the upper third of the oven and preheat to 400°F.

Put a pan of water over low heat on the back burner, ready to poach the eggs.

Peel, then grate the sweet and Yukon Gold potatoes on the large holes of a box grater. Cut the onion into small dice and add it to the potatoes with the eggs, flour, cayenne, black pepper, and salt. Mix well, set aside for 5 minutes, and mix together the Chive Crème Fraîche.

Put a large, heavy skillet over medium heat and add 1 to 2 teaspoons of oil per latke. Lightly pack a 1/3 cup measure with the mixture, then turn it out onto one hand and with both hands form a slightly flattened cake about an inch thick. Fry the latkes for 4 minutes on the first side, then flip and cook, pressing down a couple of times with the spatula, for another 4 minutes. Adjust the heat as you go along so they cook to a dark golden brown. As the latkes are ready, put them on a sheet pan. When they're all done, put them in the oven for 10 minutes to finish cooking. When they're ready, just turn off the oven and they will stay hot for at least 15 minutes. This frees you up to poach the eggs.

THE CHIVE CRÈME FRAÎCHE

1 cup crème fraîche (or sour cream)

1/2 teaspoon smoked paprika, (see Resources, page 211)

2 tablespoons snipped chives, plus more for garnish

1/2 teaspoon kosher salt

In a medium bowl, mix all the ingredients together and set aside.

THE POACHED EGGS

1 extra-large egg per latke

Bring the pan of hot water that you have going on the back burner to a simmer. Add each egg individually, giving it time to set a little, then release it from the base of the pan with a metal spatula before adding the next one. Some people add vinegar to the water to hold the whites together, but if you use

reliably fresh eggs, you won't need to. If you are cooking for a crowd, put the cooked poached eggs into a dish and cover with warm water. They will stop cooking and will hold for at least 15 minutes.

TO ASSEMBLE

When you're ready to serve, arrange some salmon on each latke. Lift each egg out with a slotted spoon, rest the spoon on a paper towel for a few seconds to drain the water. Set the egg on a latke beside the smoked salmon. Top with the Chive Crème Fraîche.

SCRAMBLED EGGS
Serves 4

In England we make scrambled eggs in a saucepan, not a skillet. The eggs themselves are delicate and creamy without a sheen of butter, making them a perfect home for spicy sausage, strong cheeses, and minced green herbs. All I know is that when friends come for the weekend they get very helpful around breakfast time and say things like, "If we make the coffee, lay the table, squeeze the orange juice, and toast the toast . . . could you make your special eggs? Please." Plan so that when the eggs are ready, you can all sit and eat them straightaway; people should wait for the eggs, not vice versa. Your guests or family can be buttering their toast in anticipation.

   8 extra-large eggs

   1/2 teaspoon freshly ground black pepper, or to taste

   1 teaspoon kosher salt (if you are going to add chorizo or a salty cheese, you might want to use less)

   3 tablespoons unsalted butter

   1/4 cup whole milk

In a large bowl whisk the eggs, pepper, and salt well. Put a heavy pan small enough so that the eggs will be at least an inch deep (a 3-quart pan is fine) over medium heat, add the butter and milk, and bring to a boil.

Pour the eggs into the pan, stir to mix, and turn the heat down low. Using a flat-bottomed wooden spatula, start scraping the base of the pan. Keep on scraping the egg off the base—please don't be impatient and turn up the heat, or the eggs will become tough. Eight eggs will take 7 or 8 minutes to scramble. If the eggs start cooking too fast, just take the pan off the heat. There might even be enough residual heat in the pan and the eggs themselves for the cooking to complete off the burner; just keep stirring till they're the way you like them. The eggs should never get very, very hot. If they do, they'll become irrevocably hard, so again, allow enough time for them to cook at a low temperature.

Note: If you're cooking many more than 8 eggs, you might find that despite your best efforts the egg on the bottom has formed a cooked brown film that you're starting to scrape up. At this point you are better off tipping the uncooked mixture into a different pan and adding another couple of whisked eggs. This has happened to me plenty of times, so don't feel discouraged—just be glad you noticed and did something about it before the eggs were full of brown bits.

SCRAMBLED EGG VARIATIONS

SCRAMBLED EGGS WITH SPICY ITALIAN SAUSAGE

2   ounces spicy Italian sausage per person

Warm the oil in a large nonstick skillet over medium-high heat. Add the sausage and fry, turning occasionally until nicely browned, about 7 minutes. Cut the sausage into slices 1/3 inch thick and add to the eggs halfway through cooking.

SCRAMBLED EGGS WITH CHEESE

3/4   ounce extra-sharp cheddar, pepper jack, or aged Gouda per person, grated

Add the cheese a couple of minutes before the eggs are ready.

SCRAMBLED EGGS WITH FRESH HERBS

2   tablespoons chopped fresh herbs per person

Use a combination of minced parsley, basil, scallions, or chives. If you have some tarragon lying around, use that too but just a little, as it's a rather domineering flavor. When the eggs are done, stir in most of the herbs, saving some to scatter over the eggs when they're plated.

GUADALAJARA HASH
NOT ILLEGAL, JUST FUN TO SAY
Serves 4 to 6 (depending on greed)

This dish is made in the oven and is just roasted sweet potatoes tossed with olive oil, hot red pepper flakes, cumin seeds, honey, and smoked paprika. It's quite an eye-opener at breakfast and is fabulous with a couple of fried or poached eggs on top. It takes a long time to develop its melting, crunchy, sticky character and can't be hurried, so I sometimes make the whole thing the night before and just crisp it up in a hot oven for 15 to 20 minutes the next morning. The greed issue is only mentioned because while recipe testing alone in my house in Connecticut, I'm sorry to say I finished off the whole lot all by myself. Unfortunately it's like the deadly Coke and popcorn movie combo—horrifyingly addictive.

2   pounds sweet potatoes

1/3   cup olive oil

1   tablespoon honey

1   teaspoon cumin seeds

1   teaspoon smoked paprika (see Resources, page 211)

1/2   teaspoon hot red pepper flakes

1   teaspoon kosher salt, or to taste

Position a rack at the top of the oven and pre-heat to 400°F.

Wash the unpeeled sweet potatoes and chop them roughly into pieces no more than 1 inch square. Stir all the ingredients together in a large bowl. Using a rubber spatula, scrape everything out onto a heavy baking sheet (my ideal container for this is a dark, metal 13- by 9-inch brownie pan) and put in the oven. After 30 minutes, turn the sweet potatoes with a metal spatula, then flip again 15 minutes later. At this point, I usually break up the sweet potatoes a bit with the spatula. Roast for another 25 minutes, with a total baking time of 1 hour and 10 minutes.

Note: This recipe can be assembled the night before and left covered in a bowl in the fridge. The next morning, stir to coat, then bake as above, adding 5 or 10 minutes cooking time because everything will be cold.

THE HOUSE IN THE MANGO TREES—TORTOLA, PART I (PART II, PAGE 72) In January of 1992, I went to live for nine months on Tortola in the British Virgin Islands. It was an island of trash and beauty, overrun by European interlopers. Old car batteries littered the roads, which were often blocked by drifts of squealing baby pigs. Soignée oceangoing yachts and their owners hung around the harbors, being polished to within an inch of their lives and chain-smoking, respectively.

Husband #2 and I had been (note the past tense) dewy-eyed about building a second home there, but construction had been limping along for well over a year.

I was in trouble: Apparently, all the problems down there were my fault, since the architect responsible had been my particular pet. We were both English and together had drooled over his vision—a trio of classical Palladian villas linked by covered walkways. They were to be perched on a tropical hillside, and the garden was to be built around five enormous mango trees. Husband #2's dollars had mysteriously evaporated, which was more under-standable when we were told the governor's house had our tiles on his roof. As it stood, we could probably have built a small town on Tortola for the cost of our three villas, which were not even close to being finished. The architect had been fired, along with the builder, the foreman and his crew. FIRED, FIRED, FIRED.

Off I was sent in early January to hire people, buy a truck, and get the house finished. ("Who, me??") The guesthouse was almost livable, so on arriving I camped there and the next morning set off in search of construction workers. Because Tortola is so small, everyone on the island knew of our plight, and by midday I owned a *Beverly Hillbillies* sort of a truck and had a gang of genial locals ready to work. The foreman and I spent a disconcerting fifteen or so minutes turning the blueprints round and round until we established which way was up . . . then building started again.

This was the life: no more aerobics classes, no more manicures. I would stay fit by hauling bricks up and down a ladder, and my nails could—and would—go to hell.

I watched *This Old House* on PBS like a hawk, looking for building tips that were relevant to our house, and became hideously opinionated. The poor foreman's eyes would roll as I explained, *"Yes, but that's not how they did it on the telly."*

We started at seven in the morning and every day, at 3:28 P.M., the men were still hammering and painting away. At 3:30, they were gone. Their lightning transit through time and space always amazed me, but the subsequent silence was nothing short of Divine. I would check the work done during the day, then with bikini, book, and beer, drive to the beach eight hundred feet below our house. I would read for a while, then drift in and out of sleep as a background of radio music, children playing, and dogs barking formed an island white noise. Later, I would swim out far enough to see our beautiful villas and wonder presciently whether my husband and I would ever live in them.

The weeks sped by. I noticed that I didn't cook anymore. I noticed that someone had written Hi! in the dust on a table; I knew I couldn't remember when I last changed my sheets.

On my drive back from the beach one evening, I passed a girl sitting on a fallen tree at the side of the road. It was an unusual sight, as no one ever walked that road; it was far too long and steep and people would wait for hours down at the beach for a ride to the top. Luckily, I had left my book at the beach and about an hour later decided to drive down and get it. The young woman was still on her tree, but was now sobbing into her skirt. She told me a garbled, hiccupy story involving a lying uncle, a promised job, and a lost suitcase. Lucy came home with me.

She guaranteed me God's blessings and divine intervention for the rest of my life—so that was a welcome perk. I thought my charitable act could work out well for both of us, but I had no idea. I'd welcomed under our roof Martha Stewart, Julia Child, and Tammy Faye Bakker, all rolled into one dynamo from Dominica.

The swearing had to stop, especially those groups of words starting with Jesus. Gooselike,

I ate three square meals a day, and the guesthouse shone so brilliantly that I hesitated to step inside, for fear of messing it up.

The workers voted Lucy snooty; she knew they all had wives and would frown on their flirtation and wag her finger formidably. Standing on a little chair, she cut any ripe mangoes she could reach from our trees and brought me a bowl of the juicy fruit with a wedge of lime every morning at six. She started a vegetable garden, which proved so excitingly fecund, that virtually every day she felt compelled to expose yet another patch of soil in which to house her watermelon, pumpkin, ginger, hot peppers—the list was endless. I had to beg her to stop digging before she undermined the foundations.

As the produce piled up, I started to eye it speculatively and decided it was time to have all the new friends I had made to dinner. There was very little fresh meat on the island, except extortionate porterhouse, for the yacht set. The trick was to go down to the fish shack, where fishermen brought their catch, and wait until something you fancied came in. The first time I went, I took a book, as I thought waiting was "downtime" and had no understanding of the activities inherent in the wait. There was the faux insouciant, jockeying for position at the top of the fishermen's gangway from the dock . . . thus attempting first dibs on their fish. There was an established group of high-class gossips who sat in the shade, drinking and defaming. Since island life would collapse in a heap without gossip and one's reputation could skyrocket with shrewdly revealed information . . . *it behooved you to loiter near that group, ears flapping.* The third activity of the fish shack was listening to the shortwave radio, which shared a shelf with bottles of hot sauce and tins of lime-scented pomade. The radio was always tuned to the BBC home service, and it gave me such delight to hear any part of a radio play or a quiz show that I passed up many a fine catch as I stood captivated by the English language.

My first dinner party was as much fun for me as it was for my friends, since I embraced the cooking of it like a long-lost friend. I became carried away with exterior decoration and draped our twenty-foot-long pergola with orange and gold saris, and from the start, the 180 proof rum punch with fresh mango puree and cane sugar made all of us amazingly jolly.

My affection for island life drove a thick wedge between Husband #2 and me. In the nine months of separation, despite his few flying visits, I had gestated a new persona and psychologically there was no going back. He took over on the island and I returned to New York, to the beginning of the life I have now. We parted at the airport, where he peeled off four twenty-dollar bills, and I think he said, "Have a good life." *I blow a big kiss to Tortola.*

GLAMOROUS FRUIT
Serves 6

The only thing simpler would be the mangoes on their own—as in the Tortola story—but Asian pears with their juicy crunch seemed like a good idea. One morning when this fruit salad was already on the table, a houseguest (who lives for fashion, style, and Marlboro red cigarettes) appeared in his Charvet robe, peered at the fruit in its glass dish, and croaked, "That looks very glamorous." So glamorous fruit it is.

2 mangoes, chilled

2 Asian pears, chilled

1 bunch perky mint, 10 of the leaves cut into fine shreds just before you need them, and the rest reserved for decoration

Peel the mangoes and cut into diagonal 3/4-inch chunks. If the Asian pears have a thin skin, you can leave it on; otherwise peel the pears before cutting. Cut the pears the same way and toss both fruits with the shredded mint. Use the rest of the bunch of mint for decoration. Happily, Asian pears don't turn brown like other pears when they are left out for a while.

Curried Egg and Pink Radish Tea Sandwiches

Homemade Mayonnaise

Cucumber and Watercress Tea Sandwiches

Rare Roast Beef Tea Sandwiches

Horseradish Cream

Sausage Rolls

Cheating Chocolate Cake

Ganache

Cardamom and Apple Cake with Chocolate Dribble

Vanilla Cake

Lemon Curd Cake

Vanilla Cupcakes

Creamy Cream Frosting

Drop Scones

Jam Tarts

Chocolate Chip Cookies to Base the Rest of Your Life On

SIMPLE FOOD ON FANCY PLATES = TEATIME

This one little word is so steeped in nostalgia for me that even though the meal itself is generally defunct, I'm inclined to start a one-woman revival movement. How could two-bite sandwiches, jam tarts, and sausage rolls ever fall from favor? The truth is that teatime flourished when women didn't work and could either summon up help or had the time themselves to put together this tempting spread.

Afternoon tea is an innately sociable occasion as we eat the other three meals whether we have guests or not; it would take a committed narcissist to conjure up drop scones and chocolate cake at teatime just for themselves. You don't need knives and forks, and you don't need to sit around a table to eat at teatime. Dream teas are either positioned in front of a fireplace with a crackling fire or under a spreading chestnut tree with wicker furniture, rugs, and Wedgwood china. Intimacy and a delicious shared guilt (the calories) prevail, and as the sugar and caffeine course through our veins, a good time is usually had by all.

TEA SANDWICHES

Everyone knows how to make a sandwich, but in order for it to earn a spot on a three-tiered silver thing or even a fancy plate, you have to think thin and you have to think small. Choose breads that are at home with their fillings. Fresh, thinly-sliced seeded rye with cream cheese and wafers of English cucumber is a totally addictive combination, as indeed are whole wheat bread with Curried Egg and Pink Radish, and pumpernickel with shaved Rare Roast Beef and Horseradish Cream. If you are feeding big, strong men who will feel silly with a tiny little sandwich, make them "club" tea sandwiches—three slices of bread with two layers of filling. That might help.

CURRIED EGG AND PINK RADISH TEA SANDWICHES

Makes 12 tea sandwiches

- 3 extra-large eggs, boiled for 7 minutes, then cooled and peeled
- 4 pink radishes, minced
- 3 tablespoons minced chives
- 1/3 cup Homemade Mayonnaise (recipe follows), or Hellmann's Mayonnaise
- 1 teaspoon curry powder
- 3/4 teaspoon kosher salt
- 1/2 teaspoon freshly ground black pepper
- 2 to 3 tablespoons unsalted butter, softened
- 6 thin slices whole wheat bread

Chop the eggs medium-fine and tip into a large bowl. Mix in the radishes, chives, mayonnaise, curry powder, salt, and pepper. Refrigerate, covered with plastic wrap, for at least an hour, or overnight.

To assemble the sandwiches, lightly butter the bread, spread EACH SLICE thinly with some filling, sandwich the slices together, trim off the crusts, and cut the sandwiches into triangles.

HOMEMADE MAYONNAISE

Makes 2 cups

I remember many years ago my friend Peter Schlesinger telling me about making mayonnaise in a food processor. I could hardly believe my ears, as he cooks with tremendous skill and attention to detail, and I would never have thought him capable of abandoning his whisk. Not only was he recommending an idiot-proof shortcut, but he also rather reluctanly told me you could use vegetable oil instead of an olive oil as it thickens better. *Sacrilege upon sacrilege.*

Well, for an everyday mayonnaise that's almost as quick as opening a jar and about a million times better—he was right. If you know your guests and can use peanut oil with impunity (allergies, etc.), that's the best choice. Otherwise, canola is fine. You'll make more mayonnaise than you need for these tea sandwiches, but it will keep for at least a week and is great as a base for a quick dip.

1 extra-large egg

1 tablespoon fresh lemon juice or aged sherry vinegar (see Resources, page 211)

1 1/2 teaspoons Dijon mustard

1 garlic clove, chopped (optional)

1/2 teaspoon kosher salt

1/4 teaspoon freshly ground black pepper

1 1/2 cups peanut or canola oil

Put the egg, lemon juice, mustard, garlic, salt, and pepper in the bowl of a food processor and blend for 20 seconds. Then slowly, while the machine is running, add the oil in a thin stream; by the time it's all in, the mayonnaise will be thick and ready to go.

CUCUMBER AND WATERCRESS TEA SANDWICHES

Makes 12 tea sandwiches

6 very thin slices seeded rye bread

1 cup cream cheese, softened

1 bunch watercress (large stems removed), chopped

1/3 English (hothouse) cucumber, very thinly sliced

Kosher salt to taste

Freshly ground black pepper to taste

Spread all the slices of bread with cream cheese, and then press some chopped water-

cress onto 3 slices and cucumber on the other 3. Salt and pepper the cucumber well and firmly press the cucumber and watercress-slices together.

I like to leave these sandwiches untrimmed, uncut, and wrapped with plastic wrap in the fridge for about an hour. The salt will draw the water out of the cucumber and encourage the watercress to relax, so when you trim the crusts and cut the sandwich into quarters, everything will hold together much better and taste sublime.

RARE ROAST BEEF TEA SANDWICHES

Makes 12 tea sandwiches

This is the original sandwich: steak between slices of bread, as requested of a manservant by the actual Earl of Sandwich in the 1700s. It was late at night, he was engrossed in a card game (winning and hungry) and didn't want to leave the table or to get his cards greasy. His easy solution caught on rather fast.

Horseradish Cream (recipe follows)

8 thin slices pumpernickel bread

8 ounces rare roast beef, thinly sliced

Kosher salt to taste

Freshly ground black pepper to taste

To assemble these sandwiches, spread the Horseradish Cream thinly on each slice of bread. Arrange a thin layer of roast beef on each slice and sprinkle with salt and pepper. Put 2 slices together to make each sandwich. Cut off the crusts and cut across twice to make 3 rectangles. *You'll create a more manly shape than a triangle.*

HORSERADISH CREAM
Makes 3/4 cup

1/3 cup packed freshly grated horseradish

1 teaspoon tarragon or white wine vinegar

1 teaspoon Dijon mustard

1/2 teaspoon kosher salt

1/2 teaspoon freshly ground black pepper

1/2 cup heavy cream, softly whipped

Use a microplane grater to grate the very fibrous horseradish, then mix the horseradish with the vinegar to keep the flavor from dissipating. Add the mustard, salt, and pepper, mix again; then fold into the whipped cream.

SAUSAGE ROLLS
Makes 8 sausage rolls
(or 16 mini-sausage rolls)

I wish there were a better name, as these two words don't exactly conjure up the ageless nobility that English people comprehend when talking of pork sausages rolled in puff pastry. Sausage rolls are found in the most austere Yorkshire farmhouse and make it all the way to Buckingham Palace. In fact, they have a universal (in England, anyway) appeal, and maybe even a little magic in them. They are hardly fat-free but seem feather-light as your teeth bite through with no resistance (due to the skinless sausages) and flakes of pastry drift weightlessly down. Serve with Dijon mustard, or try the less aggresive Amora mustard (see Resources, page 211).

1 package frozen puff pastry (usually about 16 ounces) preferably defrosted overnight in the refrigerator

1 egg, whisked, for glazing

1 package Jones precooked skinless pork sausages or other breakfast sausages

Kosher salt

Position a rack in the top third of the oven and preheat to 400°F.

Roll a piece of puff pastry to 12 by 6 inches and cut into eight 3-inch squares. Use the egg wash to brush the top 1/2 inch of each square. Place a sausage along the bottom edge and roll it up, ending with the seam underneath. Brush the top of each roll with egg wash, sprinkle with salt, and decide if you want large or small sausage rolls. Cut them in half for smaller ones. Put on an ungreased baking sheet and, with a sharp knife, make 2

or 3 small diagonal cuts on top. Bake for 15 minutes, or until golden brown. Remove from the oven, cool for a couple of minutes, and serve warm or at room temperature.

CAKES: PLAIN OR FANCY

I love looking through old cookbooks and finding the headings "Plain Cakes" and "Fancy Cakes." How easy life would be if everything was identified so simply. Our choices are limitless nowadays—all the permutations of flours, nuts, leavenings, liquids, fats, fruits, and chocolates can make you weary of unnecessary invention.

There is one caveat however; a plain cake is standing on the dock alone with no blowsy buddies like raspberries, rum, or silver balls (the sometime accomplices of a fancy cake). This is the time, if you've ever had imitation vanilla or any other flavoring, to wing it into the garbage; it will not do. A plain cake's lingering mystique comes from pure, unsalted butter, organic eggs with a Gauguin yolk, sea salt (no iodine), and vanilla that has had, in its early life, a nice tropical view.

CHEATING CHOCOLATE CAKE

Makes one 9-inch layer cake

This cake is so easy, a five-year-old could make it, and it's very, very quick, so you could almost have it ready in less time than it takes to actually heat the oven. Hence the cheating. However, it has all the fine qualities that I look for in a plain cake—it's toothsome, damp, and dark. It's the cake we rely on in the catering company when a call comes in from a panicked secretary who's forgotten to order his or her boss's birthday cake. We calm the caller, and run for the cocoa. Of course, we could go out and BUY a cake, but that would really be cheating. When we're in a rush, rather than baking one large cake it's quicker to make two halves and jam them (literally) together. The icing we usually use (see the Ganache recipe on page 58) should be called "Lucifer's" as it's wickedly divine.

THE DRY INGREDIENTS

3/4 cup cocoa (see Resources, page 211)

2 cups granulated sugar

1 3/4 cups Heckers or King Arthur all-purpose flour

1 1/2 teaspoons baking powder

1 1/2 teaspoons baking soda

1 teaspoon kosher salt

THE WET INGREDIENTS

1 cup buttermilk

2 extra-large eggs

1/2 cup vegetable oil, plus more for greasing the pans

2 teaspoons pure vanilla extract

1 cup boiling water

Position a rack in the middle of the oven and preheat to 350°F. Grease two 9-inch cake pans and line the bases with parchment paper. Set aside.

Sift all the dry ingredients together in a large bowl. Add the buttermilk, eggs, oil, and vanilla, and whisk to combine. Add the boiling water and whisk to incorporate well. Pour the batter into the prepared pans and weigh each filled pan, adjusting the amount of batter so both weigh the same.

Bake 30 to 35 minutes, or until a toothpick inserted in the center comes out clean. Cool in the pans for 10 minutes, then turn out onto a wire rack. Remove the parchment. Turn one cake right side up; that will be the top layer. Cool completely. You can make this cake the day before serving, sandwich it with jam, and keep it covered in the fridge. Leave the cake at room temperature for an hour if you plan to cover it with Ganache (recipe follows).

GANACHE
Makes 2 cups

1 cup heavy cream

10 ounces semisweet chocolate (Valrhona, Tobler, or Ghirardelli brands), chopped fine

Heat the heavy cream in a small saucepan over medium heat until little bubbles appear around the edges. Take the pan off the heat and immediately add the chocolate; shake the pan to submerge the chocolate and leave it to melt for a couple of minutes. Using a

small whisk, stir gently to mix the chocolate to a smooth cream. Don't beat the mixture or you'll get unwanted bubbles and diminish the glossy finish. In fact, I usually use a rubber spatula for the last few strokes and to clean up around the edge.

Set aside for 20 to 30 minutes (depending on the heat of your kitchen) to thicken to a spreadable consistency. The edge will thicken sooner than the middle so carefully stir through a few times as it's cooling to keep it smooth. If you haven't already done so, sandwich the cakes together with your favorite jam. (The raspycran from Beth's Farm Kitchen, see Resources, page 211, goes particularly well with the chocolate.) Then with the help of a wide spatula, lift the cake onto a cake plate and set on a lazy Susan to be iced.

Pour the thickened Ganache in a wide ribbon around the circumference of the cake and with the help of a metal spatula, push it gently over the edge; it should fall in thick waves, but not run off completely. Fill in the middle and, using the spatula, swirl the Ganache into luscious billows. If you haven't got a lazy Susan and plan to ice even one more cake, you have to go shopping. *A lazy Susan makes it so much easier, and easy is what we like.*

I have a weakness for silver balls; they are shiny to look at and crunchy to eat. If you sprinkle some in the middle, you're on your way to the fancy cake department. The cake in the photograph on page 56 is decorated with crystallized violet petals (see Resources, page 211) which are incredibly beautiful against the shiny brown icing.

CARDAMOM AND APPLE CAKE WITH CHOCOLATE DRIBBLE

Serves 12

There's a lot of discussion about food and how to make it in the catering company but I don't have time to hang out and play nearly as much as I would like with the other cooks. HOWEVER, one weekend I found the time evaporating before a dinner for which I had offered to bring a cake. It was for a new friend's eighty-fourth birthday.

I stormed into the kitchen in a tearing rush and started softening butter in the microwave before I really knew what I was doing; I took two steps to the KitchenAid mixer and began the cake that I could probably make in a coma—batter on the bottom and fresh plums on the top. *"STOP, wait,"* (me talking) *"could we BE a little more interesting?"* Surely eighty-four years demand novelty and consideration. Well, it was the week of the cardamom fetish so a powerful streusel was flung together and scattered thickly on the batter. Plums were out of season in the walkin refrigerator but Granny Smith apples were not, so this utterly fabulous cake came into being with love and a certain amount of good luck.

I made a large cake because I knew the apples would need at least an hour in the oven to cook through to a melting softness. It's very good the next day, so you'll be glad of the surplus.

THE STREUSEL

- 1/2 cup light brown sugar
- 2 tablespoons cinnamon
- 1 tablespoon cardamom seeds (see Resources, page 211), finely ground in a spice grinder
- 1 cup walnut halves, chopped or pulsed medium in a food processor

Mix all the ingredients together in a small bowl and set aside. One quarter cup of this streusel is great tossed through with the topping for a peach and ginger crisp.

THE CAKE

- 2 cups Heckers or King Arthur all-purpose flour
- 2 teaspoons baking powder
- 1/2 teaspoon kosher salt
- 16 tablespoons (2 sticks) unsalted butter, softened
- 2 cups sugar, plus 1 tablespoon for sprinkling
- 4 extra-large eggs
- 2 teaspoons pure vanilla extract
- 5 Granny Smith apples, peeled, quartered and cored
- 2 tablespoons fresh lemon juice
- 1 teaspoon cinnamon

Position a rack in the upper third of the oven and preheat to 350°F. Grease a 12-inch diameter cake pan or a 9- by 13-inch brownie pan; line the base with parchment paper and set aside.

Sift the flour, baking powder, and salt and set aside. In an electric mixer fitted with a balloon attachment, cream the butter for 3 minutes, add the 2 cups sugar, and beat for another 3 minutes until light and fluffy. Add the eggs and vanilla and beat again for 3 minutes. Remove the bowl from the mixer and fold in the flour mixture.

Spread half the batter on the base of the pan and sprinkle on all the streusel. Cover as best you can with the balance of the batter; then place the apples clockways and face down, around the edge, then in the center. Sprinkle on the lemon juice, cinnamon, and the 1 tablespoon of sugar. Bake for 60 to 70 minutes, or until a toothpick inserted comes out clean. Cool in the pan, then run a small, sharp knife around the edge to release the cake and turn out onto a flat cookie sheet. Peel off the paper and turn back onto a cake plate.

VANILLA BEANS

Eat the cake just as it is, or drip runny chocolate ganache (1/4 cup heavy cream scalded, then mixed with 2 1/2 ounces chopped semi-sweet chocolate) over the top à la Jackson Pollock, letting the chocolate dribble over the edge where it will. *This is a sexy female sort of a cake and can't be constrained.*

VANILLA CAKE
Makes one 12-inch loaf cake

This gorgeous cake can do no wrong. I slip it to guests with a "Have a little slice of cake" and after a few bites, they become thoughtful and then pronounce, *"You know, this is my favorite kind of cake"*. The pure vanilla shines through beautifully since it's not masked by a sour cream or buttermilk twang.

- 1 cup sugar
- 2 vanilla beans or 2 teaspoons pure vanilla extract
- 3 extra-large eggs
- 1 cup heavy cream
- 1 1/2 cups cake flour, preferably White Lily (see Resources, page 211) or Gold Medal
- 1 1/2 teaspoons baking powder
- 1/2 teaspoon kosher salt
- 1/4 cup superfine or granulated sugar for dusting the top

Position a rack in the middle of the oven and preheat to 350°F. Grease a 12-inch loaf pan or a 10-inch round cake pan, and line the base with parchment paper, then set aside.

Put the sugar in a small bowl. Slice the vanilla beans lengthwise and scrape out the sticky black seeds with the back of a small knife; then, using your fingertips, rub the seeds in with the sugar.

In an electric mixer beat the eggs and the vanilla sugar you've created, (if using the vanilla extract, add it now) until it's pale and thick, about 5 minutes. Transfer the mixture to a wide bowl. Whip the cream in the same bowl with the electric mixer till soft peaks form. Turn it out onto the egg and sugar mixture. Sift on the flour, baking powder, and salt, then gently fold all together.

Turn the batter into the prepared pan and smooth the top. Dust the top of the cake with the superfine sugar and bake for 40 minutes, or until a toothpick inserted in the center comes out clean. Remove the cake from the oven and cool for 15 minutes.

Fold a clean kitchen towel and lay it over the top of the cake to protect the delicate layer of sugary crust, then turn the cake out onto a cookie sheet. Peel off the paper and turn the cake back onto a rack to cool completely, removing the towel.

If (quite unusually) this cake lasts long enough to become stale . . . toast a slice and eat it slathered with butter and jam, or use it to build a trifle with strawberries, rhubarb, custard, and hazelnuts.

SANDY AND THE LEMON CAKE STORY In my early days of starting to cater again, with the sole purpose not being carted off to the poor house (a place mentioned a lot by my father, who had four expensive daughters), I could hardly bear to do anything that wasn't directly relevant to my burgeoning business. I ate as I cooked—a deadly practice—and succumbed to sleep only when there was categorically nothing else I could do before the morning. I used to wander around the garden at midnight with a flashlight, picking flowers for the next day's Richard Avedon or Irving Penn shoot and then fall out of bed at about four A.M. to start making horseradish sauce and pastry.

I think it was a little dramatic, and with a bit more organization I could have had several more hours of sleep, but it did feel as though I was trying really hard and would ultimately be rewarded. Every scrap of food I made seemed very important, so this luscious lemon cake was coaxed along with TLC. On the morning in question, I had made a lovely cake that had risen well, and the lemon curd on top had caramelized handsomely. I'd put it to cool in the kitchen on a rack near the sink. I had decided that an espresso crème caramel would be interesting for lunch the next day, so that had been made earlier and was also out cooling, this time on the kitchen's center island.

It was a Saturday in June and my children, Joe and Sam, had come up from Manhattan for the weekend. They had brought Sandy, a supremely amiable golden retriever, with them for a look at country things like fireflies and bats.

No one was awake yet, so I drove up the road to get some milk and the newspaper. I was gone for less than ten minutes. When I returned, Sandy met me at the front door in an expansively good mood; she was grinning from ear to ear and wagging her rear half wildly. I was pleased to see her too and gave her a big kiss, and noticing a nice new shampoo (?) on her that smelled of . . . LEMON. I took two steps to the kitchen door and saw the evidence. "Sandy!" I thundered, "What have you done . . . you horrible, HORRIBLE dog."

Sandy heard her name and wagged even harder. The front of the lemon cake was gone, and the back, evidently just beyond the reach of her teeth, was sort of licked to death and all slobbery and mashed. Of the crème caramel, there was no sign. I heard a gasping, snorting noise behind me and turned to find Joe and Sam in their pajamas, clinging to each other with hands clamped over their mouths, making feeble efforts not to explode with laughter. "It's not funny," I said furiously, but at that moment Sandy let out a loud fart, and we all collapsed in hysterical giggles and rolled around on the floor with some crumbs and the delighted dog. Please take more care of this cake than I did.

LEMON CURD CAKE
Serves 10 to 12

THE POWER LEMON CURD

- 1/2 cup sugar
- Pinch of kosher salt
- Zest of 3 lemons
- 1/2 cup lemon juice
- 4 extra-large egg yolks
- 2 extra-large whole eggs
- 7 tablespoons unsalted butter at room temperature

In a medium-size nonstick or nonreactive saucepan, add the sugar, salt, and lemon zest and juice, and whisk until smooth. Then add the egg yolks and whole eggs and quickly

whisk well. Set over medium-low heat and cook, stirring pretty much constantly until the mixture starts to bubble around the edges (about 8 minutes). Then add the butter in little lumps, stirring after each addition, and simmer gently. *(No boiling, as the molten mixture can cause quite a burn if it splats onto your hand.)* Stir for about 5 minutes, until the mixture thickens well. Transfer it to a small shallow bowl and cover with plastic wrap pressed onto the surface while the mixture is still hot; set aside to cool. Once it's cool, you can use it for the Lemon Curd Cake or transfer it to a plastic container, cover the surface as before, and store in the fridge for a week or in the freezer for up to 2 months.

THE CAKE

- 1 1/2 cups Heckers or King Arthur all-purpose flour
- 1 1/2 teaspoons baking powder
- 3/4 teaspoon kosher salt
- 12 tablespoons (1 1/2 sticks) unsalted butter, at room temperature
- 1 1/2 cups sugar
- 3 extra-large eggs
- 3 tablespoons finely grated lemon zest

Position a rack in the middle of the oven and preheat to 350°F. Grease a 9-inch springform pan with vegetable oil.

Sift the flour, baking powder, and salt together and set aside. Using an electric mixer with the

balloon whisk attachment, beat the butter until creamy and pale, about 5 minutes. Add the sugar and beat for 3 minutes. While the sugar is fluffing up, break the eggs into a bowl and whisk to blend. Gradually pour the eggs into the mixture and beat for another 2 minutes. Scrape the sides and base of the bowl a couple times to make sure everything is well incorporated.

Remove the bowl from the mixer, stir in the lemon zest, add the dry ingredients, and fold in gently until just a little flour is still visible.

Spread half the cake batter on the base of the pan. Cover with half of the lemon curd, keeping just shy of the perimeter. Spoon on the remaining batter somewhat randomly, then drop 3 large spoonfuls of the lemon curd on top of the batter. Shimmy the cake back and forth to level the curd and batter and create a marbling effect.

Bake for 45 to 50 minutes or until a toothpick

inserted in the cake comes out clean and the lemon curd on top has turned a rich golden brown. If the curd is browning too much, lay a sheet of aluminum foil over the pan.

Let the cake cool completely in the pan. Then run a small sharp knife around the circumference. Release and remove the sides of the springform. Run a large, sharp unserrated knife under the cake to loosen it. Then use the knife blade to help slide it onto a cake plate. You can EITHER dust with confectioners' sugar (with or without a pile of raspberries) OR leave the cake plain so the lemon curd shows. DECISIONS, DECISIONS.

CUPCAKE COMMENTS As I write this book, New York City is still in the grip of cupcake fever; it all started in 1988 with the Cupcake Cafe which made delicious little cakes with riotous buttercream flowers in colors so intense they looked like Fauve paintings and sometimes left you with a blue tongue. Then came Magnolia Bakery, a busy corner of homemade heaven, offering cakes (and particularly cupcakes) with that slightly naïve simplicity which usually marks an earnest young cook's first attempt at a sponge.

Cupcakes have entered the mainstream and can be found preening with upward mobility and masquerading as dessert on the poshest uptown tables. Their little heads are swathed with sugar and spangled with dragées; crème fraîche and expensive berries are their companions. *I think it's fair to say that cupcakes have arrived.*

VANILLA CUPCAKES
Makes 12 cupcakes

I have tested and adapted what seems like every recipe in the world, looking for a tender but characterful vanilla cupcake, and the only one I've really fallen for is made with lard. If you balk at the idea of lard, then use Crisco, but lard is just the best: These cupcakes are absolute perfection. In my catering kitchen we use the Cheating Chocolate Cake batter (see recipe, page 57) for chocolate cupcakes.

1 1/4 cups cake flour, preferably White Lily (see Resources, page 211) or Gold Medal

3/4 teaspoon baking soda

3/4 teaspoon baking powder

3 extra-large egg whites, at room temperature

1/2 teaspoon kosher salt

1 cup sugar

6 tablespoons lard, at room temperature (or substitute Crisco), plus more for greasing the muffin tin

2 extra-large egg yolks

1 teaspoon pure vanilla extract

1 cup whole milk

Creamy Cream Frosting (recipe follows)

Crystallized roses and dragées for going completely over the top (see Resources, page 211)

Position a rack in the middle of the oven and preheat to 350°F. Grease a muffin tin or line the tin with paper cases and set aside.

Sift the flour, baking soda, and baking powder into a large bowl and set aside. Using an electric mixer with the balloon whisk, whip the egg whites with the salt until doubled in size. Add 1 tablespoon of the sugar and beat for another minute. Transfer to a wide bowl and set aside. Using the same mixing bowl and the electric mixer, cream the lard with the rest of the sugar, then add the egg yolks and vanilla and beat well. Fold the whites into the egg yolk mixture. Don't worry if it looks all grainy; it's OK. Fold in half of the dry ingredients, then half the milk, then repeat. Pour the batter into the muffin tins and bake for 18 minutes, or until a toothpick inserted in the center comes out clean. Allow the cupcakes to rest for 5 minutes in the tin, then tip them out onto a rack. Ice when they're completely cool.

CREAMY CREAM FROSTING
Makes 3 cups

8 tablespoons (1 stick) unsalted butter, at room temperature

8 ounces cream cheese, softened

4 cups confectioners' sugar, sifted

1 teaspoon pure vanilla extract

4 teaspoons fresh lemon juice

1/2 teaspoon rose water (optional) (see Resources, page 211)

In an electric mixer fitted with the paddle attachment, beat the butter with the cream cheese, scraping the sides of the bowl down often, until the mixture is smooth and lump-free. Add the sugar, vanilla, lemon juice, and the optional rose water, and beat until well mixed. (A tablespoon of dark rum is a great alternative to the rose water.)

CREAMY PASTEL FROSTING

This is the frosting we use for the pretty pink cupcake in the above photograph. If you want to tint the frosting, add the coloring very gradually—it's IRREVOCABLE and, once it's in, obviously can't come back out. And it's so boring to have to make more white frosting.

TASTING THE MEMORY STORY My sisters and I have an unnatural reverence for these scones, as they are the only recipe we have in our mother's handwriting. They're sturdy little things that look nothing like scones as we know them but rather like dollar pancakes with more body, a tender bite, and a memorable flavor.

We would gather in the kitchen on a Sunday afternoon around 4:00 P.M. for tea. The plan was always to bring a dozen warm drop scones to the tea table in a folded linen napkin but despite our mother's best efforts at decorum, I never remember seeing more than a few together at a time. As Mummy cooked the scones on the hotplate of our Aga—a huge coal burning stove with five ovens—my three older sisters would wait like vultures, then greedily burn their fingertips as they picked the drop scones up almost before they were ready. They'd slather on salted butter and homemade strawberry jam and eat them with the melted butter dripping off their elbows. I did rather better, as I was usually balanced on my mother's hip and was handed plenty of drop scones by her. I wasn't allowed anywhere near the hot-plate but *(it being 1949) did have to dodge the cigarette hanging from her pretty lips.*

DROP SCONES
Makes 15 to 20 scones

- 1 cup Heckers or King Arthur all-purpose flour
- 1 teaspoon baking soda
- 1/2 teaspoon baking powder
- 1/2 teaspoon cream of tartar
- 1/4 cup sugar
- 2 tablespoons unsalted butter, melted
- 1 extra-large egg
- 1 tablespoon honey
- 1/2 cup whole milk

Sift the flour, baking soda, baking powder, cream of tartar, and sugar into a deep bowl and set aside. When you're ready to cook the scones, heat a griddle well and brush the sur- face with butter. Add the egg, honey, and milk to the dry ingredients and whisk to mix. Drop the batter by tablespoonfuls on the medium-hot griddle, and when bubbles appear and start to pop (after about 3 min-utes), turn and cook another minute or two. The scones should be a chestnutty brown rather than golden brown. Eat standing up, with salted butter and strawberry jam.

PASTRY POLICY FOR TARTS AND PIES

1 For really crisp pastry, only use unbleached high-gluten flour like Heckers or King Arthur all-purpose—not cake flour.

2 You should see 1/4-inch freckles of butter on the underside of the plastic bag after the dough is compacted. If you can't, try fewer pulses in the food processor the next time you make this pastry since you need the little butter lumps to help make the pastry flaky.

the sisters:

Gaynor *Andra* *Serena* *Beth*

Jenny *Charles*

3 Let the dough rest for at least two hours and preferably overnight.

4 Always make sure there's enough flour under the dough so it can roll out freely. If it gets stuck to the countertop, it could stretch, then shrink in the heat of the oven and might cook unevenly or, even worse, crack.

5 Keep the dusting of flour on the surface of the dough to a minimum—just enough so the rolling pin doesn't stick.

6 Don't turn the pastry dough over and over; it's important to roll only on one side.

7 If the edge of the dough develops deep cracks, pinch it together, give the dough a half turn, and roll it from another direction.

8 If your kitchen is very warm and the dough is starting to get too soft, slide a flat cookie sheet under the rolled-out dough and transfer it to the refrigerator for five to ten minutes.

9 Make sure your oven is calibrated correctly. An accurate high heat when you first put the pastry in the oven is vital.

JAM TARTS
Makes about 18 tarts

(For 9 tarts, cut the dough in half before you roll it out and freeze one half for another day.)

For this recipe I like pastry with no sugar, cooked to a dangerous crispness, and filled with jams and citrus curds that are not too sweet. My friend Beth has a line of jams (see Resources, page 211) that she makes on a farm in upstate New York and sells at greenmarkets around Manhattan. They are equal to any great homemade jams I've ever tasted, and she has a West Highland White Terrier as do I. So, in my book . . . Beth rules.

I pretty much love all of Beth's jams, but my favorites for jam tarts are raspycran, gingered

BETH AND HER
DOG JAMS

pear, strawberry rhubarb, and apricot. I had always baked the pastry shells blind, as in empty shells lined with paper and filled with dried beans for these tarts, but one day I envisioned SQUARE tarts. I saw little squares of pastry fitted into a mini muffin tin with another tin set in on top, thereby avoiding the chore of all that paper and bean nonsense.

So we tried it, and then we all stood and watched as after fifteen minutes of baking, Mauro, my intrepid head cook, eased off the top muffin tin. Would the shells be broken, burnt, misshapen? No Way, Jose . . . only absolutely perfect.

2 1/2 cups all-purpose flour, plus extra for rolling out the dough

1 teaspoon kosher salt

16 tablespoons (2 sticks) cold unsalted butter, cut into 1/2-inch cubes

1/2 cup iced cold water (filled to the rim)

3/4 cup jam or citrus curd of your choice

Position a rack in the middle of the oven and preheat to 425°F.

Have ready 2 mini muffin tins (see Resources, page 211), ungreased. Put the flour and salt in the bowl of a food processor, add the butter, and pulse 10 times. Pour in the water in a steady stream as you pulse another 10 times. Set the crumbs aside for 5 minutes, then tip them into a baggie and gently but firmly compress into a 3/4-inch-thick rectangle. Refrigerate for at least 2 hours, or overnight.

Allow the dough to sit out for 15 minutes to soften slightly before rolling. Put the dough on a work surface. Dust the top with flour, and sprinkle a good handful of flour underneath, then roll out to a $1/8$-inch-thick rectangle and cut into 3-inch squares. Fit one square into each ungreased mini muffin tin, leaving the 4 corners out flat; nestle another tin on top and bake for 15 minutes. Remove from the oven and turn the temperature down to 350°F. Allow the shells to rest for a minute, carefully take off the top tin, then fill each shell with 2 teaspoons of jam. Bake for another 10 minutes. Since it's easy to burn your mouth on cooked jam (it stays too hot to eat for at least half an hour), put the tarts out of sight of all humans—not just children—until the jam has cooled down.

CHOCOLATE CHIP COOKIES—TORTOLA, PART II So I called my best friend, Linda, and asked her to pick me up at Kennedy Airport, as I would be arriving back from Tortola solo, with just eighty dollars (and a dream). Because my marriage had gone down in flames, her husband came too, in a display of manly support, which made me feel fractionally safer.

The most disconcerting thing when I got home was that, while I was away, my dogs had bonded with the housekeeper and were not as ecstatic to see me as I was to see them. I had to discuss life quite firmly with both of them in turn until they reverted to their routine of doting attention that was our previous mutual habit.

Being home was all very exciting for about twenty-four hours, as there were continuous phone calls and visits from scandalized friends who needed to be brought up to date. The married ones experienced a frisson of fear (concerning their own futures), but nevertheless, bravely demanded a full frontal account of the breakup. At the twenty-fifth hour, it all got terribly boring and I started considering my nonexistent finances. I examined my tatty old Smythson's address book, in search of catering clients who might want a hot meal; I found a few who actually did, but not for a while . . . *so I would have to improvise.*

I had sixty-three dollars left after grandly paying for the airport parking and buying treats to bribe the dogs back on track.

I clearly remember sitting on the back deck, looking at the view and wondering what to do, when a virtual chocolate chip cookie popped up in front of my face and reminded me of its "continent-wide" appeal. "This is America, dear," it said. "I can solve your immediate problems in the snap of a crispy cookie."

I called the local fancy market and asked if they would be interested in buying some homemade cookies. Without missing a beat, the owner said, "Sure, and bring some with nuts, too." I was amazed—indeed it was America, and an entrepreneur would never go hungry (not if I could help it anyway). I felt all misty about my adopted country and considered that in England, I would probably have been living in a ditch within a month, having to learn tramp art . . .

Warming to the plan . . . (how bad could it be?) . . . I would become adept at jumping on slow-moving freight trains and "riding the rails" to seaside resorts, where I would sell my charming little boxes and picture frames made out of matches to tourists. I could probably requisition the other tramps to help distribute them, we could divide up the towns . . .

DO PULL YOURSELF TOGETHER! I snapped at myself as I arrived at the automatic door of the local A&P to buy the chocolate chips, etc.

I wandered the aisles, wondering. Should I go for broke, almost literally, and buy the real Tahitian vanilla (?) or could I get away with . . . absolutely not. My conscience shook its busy little head. Must I get walnut halves, invisible and expensive in a can (?) or would the rather crumbly, chopped pieces in a cellophane bag do. NO . . . they would not. Chocolate chips or uneven chunks chopped from Swiss chocolate wrapped in dark brown paper—that wasn't hard. *I stood there like an ambitious suitor in Harry Winston, mentally calculating the bottom line.*

As I walked back to my car, I jubilantly knew that under the circumstances, my shopping bags held the best the A&P had to offer. If these cookies weren't sublime, it would be the work of the devil. In an ambitious fit, I made four times the recipe (240 cookies) and while the first lot baked, I did some math.

They cost twenty-two point something cents each to make. I could sell them for seventy-five cents each (Westchester, you know), so I would make about 250 percent profit . . . I thought. I did this calculation over and over, as it seemed too good to be true. In my present state of enlightenment, I recognize that I didn't consider any expenses other than the raw ingredients, but such a dizzying profit margin was so exciting to me at the time that I'm quite glad I didn't know enough to deflate my own bubble.

I found a totally inappropriate antique Japanese basket, artfully arranged sixty cookies in a spiral and took them up to the market. Got cash in hand—how fabulous was that—went home and waited for them to call me when they needed more. Which they did . . . two hours later!

"Hey . . . what'cha put in those cookies? The customers would buy one, eat it on the way to their car, and come right back for six more. Someone even got on the highway . . . and was late where they were goin', but said they just had to get more. I tell you, Serena, we're pretty excited up here."

It was a pivotal moment. I felt a wild euphoria such as a prospector might when, with one swing of his pickaxe, he reveals a golden twinkle in the rock. Did this mean I could now support myself for the first time in my life?

Independence looked like a possibility. And so it proved to be.

CHOCOLATE CHIP COOKIES
TO BASE THE REST OF YOUR LIFE ON
Makes 60

Dear Maida Heatter provided the perfect recipe in her seminal *Book of Great Chocolate Desserts*. I've minutely tweaked.

To make these cookies really well, please try to buy exactly the right ingredients. The flour, salt, butter, eggs, walnuts, and chocolate should—if humanly possible—all be as I've indicated. Then, if they aren't the best chocolate chip cookies you've ever tasted, Maida and I will just give up.

- 8 ounces (2 sticks) unsalted Land o'Lakes butter, well softened
- 3/4 cup sugar
- 3/4 cup light brown sugar
- 1 teaspoon pure vanilla extract
- 2 extra-large eggs
- 2 1/4 cups un-sifted Heckers or King Arthur all-purpose flour
- 1 teaspoon baking soda
- 1 1/4 teaspoons kosher salt
- 12 ounces (2 cups) semisweet or bittersweet chocolate, cut into 1/4-inch chunks (see Note 1)
- 8 ounces (2 generous cups) walnut halves, UNCHOPPED (see Note 2)

Using an electric mixer fitted with the balloon attachment, cream the butter until light and fluffy—about 5 minutes. Add both sugars and the vanilla and beat for 5 minutes, scraping down the sides of the bowl as needed. Add the eggs and beat again for 3 minutes. At slow speed, add half the flour and beat until incorporated, then add the remaining flour, the baking soda, and the salt, beating slowly until just mixed. Remove the mixing bowl from the machine and fold in the chocolate chunks and the walnuts. Cover the cookie dough with plastic wrap and refrigerate for at least two hours, or preferably overnight.

Position two racks to divide the oven in thirds and preheat to 375°F. Line two cookie sheets with parchment paper and set aside.

When you come to form the cookies, have at hand a small bowl of cool water. If the dough has been in the fridge overnight, it will be fairly solid. Turn the whole mixture out and break into three or four large sections so you can more easily break off small pieces. Dampen your hands lightly in the cool water, then with your fingers, scoop up 1/8 to 1/4 cup of dough, depending on the size you want the cookies. (I much prefer to use fingers rather than an ice-cream scoop to pick up the dough. The scoop will cut through the walnuts and make the cookies look more commercial.) Roll the dough quickly and lightly between your palms to form a rough ball, then slightly flatten the ball. Place the cookies on cookie sheets 1 1/2 inches apart. Dampen your hands again and rinse as needed. Bake the cookies for 12 to 15 minutes, or until the edges are golden brown, reversing the cookie sheets top to bottom and back to front

halfway through baking. Slide the cookies (still on the parchment paper) onto a cooling rack and when completely cool, store un-refrigerated in an airtight container. The dough can be well wrapped and frozen for up to a month.

Note 1: I have made these cookies using all kinds of chocolate—Lindt bittersweet or Cadbury Royal Dark or Dairy Milk, which are slab chocolates; and Nestlé or Ghirardelli chocolate chips—and I also once experimented with butterscotch morsels. The cookies were very sweet but unfortunately a HUGE hit with kids. *I'd say you couldn't possibly go wrong.*

Note 2: If you want cookies without nuts, just increase the chocolate by half.

HORS D'OEUVRES

Curried Chicken Rolled in Toasted Coconut

Shrimp Toast with Caramelized Plum and
Ginger Dip

Salmon Gravlax Tartare
on Crisp Potato Slices

Pepper-Crusted Steak with Horseradish
Cream on Grilled Garlic Crostini

Katy's Dates with Ancho Chili Oil

Black or Green Olivada

Parmesan, Rosemary, and Walnut Shortbread

Sun-Dried Tomato Pesto

COCKTAILS

The Passionate Screw

The Pink Bitch

Clicquot Rico

The Smart Blond

Brian's TKO Punch

The Rope Burn

Pimm's Cup

THE SENSORY JUGGLING ACT—SIGHT, SOUND, SMELL, TASTE, TOUCH
LIGHTING

You can make any room glamorous with a clever combination of lights on dimmers and well-placed votives or groups of candles. Their reflection in mirrors, glass vases, and the glasses on the bar will distract people's attention from a possible damp spot on the ceiling or a threadbare carpet. If you don't have anything you'd prefer to hide, the right lighting will only enhance the lovely stuff you actually do have.

Lights alone, however dim, don't do the whole job, and a welter of candles all on their own tend to look like a scary, human sacrifice sex den to me. The big deal with candles is not so much the light they shed but their flickering flames and shadows. The pockets of light and the corners that can be romanticized by candles could be played with the evening before so you can get it right then and know that at least the lights are taken care of. Make sure you do your testing at the same time of day that your guests are due to arrive, and let any pillar candles burn down a bit before you blow them out—the flame always looks better when it glows from within the candle. You'll find that rearranging groups of candles until you know they're in just the right spot will make you feel like your own set designer. Putting a little water in the bottom of a votive candle holder makes the melted candle easier to remove the next day. If pillar candles are resting on a surface that might get damaged by hot wax (a saucer often isn't big enough to hold all the melted wax), put two or three pillar candles of varying heights on a tray and cover the base with flower petals. I usually keep the lights a little brighter for the first half hour, especially as people are arriving and introductions are being made, and then as the guests get settled in and more relaxed, the lights on dimmers can go down a bit.

MUSIC

There's nothing worse than having to shout over the music. You know the volume has been too high when the first sound out of your mouth the next morning is a wheezy croak. Get some DJ-wannabe friend to adjust the volume as needed—it will probably be the opposite of the lights, low at the beginning as people are arriving and then turned up as the voices accumulate. No big deal. If you are even faintly technical . . . or know a willing twelve-year-old, you can burn your own CDs. You'll never have a song you don't like and can just put the CDs on at the beginning of the party and relax. If you plan to be loud, discuss it with the neighbors.

THE NOSE

Having been catering for a long time, I occasionally get a client who doesn't want the food to smell. (In England, smell is an all-round word, as in "that smells delicious" or "that smells horrible." We don't really say "aroma"

or "odor" much.) The wish for food not to smell is a mystery to me. I could suggest a slice of cucumber with some nice minced lettuce on top with a speck of parsley for decoration, but what the other hors d'oeuvres would be, I really don't know. I like it when the food announces itself—there's nothing like a piece of hot Parmesan shortbread topped with Sun-dried Tomato Pesto to get your guests' taste buds revved up. I love to put a layer of warm cumin seeds, black peppercorns, or star anise on a tray for an appropriate hors d'oeuvre and then, as it passes, the spicy fragrance wafts all around most tantalizingly.

Scented candles can be the most delicious thing, or verge on being repellent. When I first visited America in 1968, Husband #1 and I lived in New Haven and craft-ridden gift shops reeking of strawberry or eggnog scented candles abounded. I had to hold my breath as I passed them, and I still find that particular kind of smell VERY DISRUPTIVE, certainly not something you would want to be enveloped by if there was food around. Having said that, I do love the scented candles listed on page 211; they are all subtle and chic, and will add an air of sophistication to any living room.

TASTE

I try to keep hors d'oeuvres bite-size—we've all bitten into something at a cocktail party and found you just couldn't get all the way through, so you had to stuff the whole thing in your mouth and nod in agreement a lot for the next minute. In my life, it's always at exactly that point when someone says, "And what do you think, Serena?" Everyone turns to me in anticipation of a smart remark, but all I can do is helplessly chew away and point at my cheek.

When inventing a new hors d'oeuvre, aim for a blast of flavor with every morsel. You can be a little less circumspect with your seasoning than usual, as you're dealing with a tiny mouthful, which only has fifteen *seconds* to become famous. Katy's Dates with Ancho Chili Oil (see recipe, page 87) are so packed with flavor that if you ate six in a row, they might start to taste too sweet, too salty, too spicily hot and herbal; BUT one or two—OK three—with a glass of Sangiovese, and all's right with the world.

Stock up on ice and try to keep the cold drinks cold. Remember, never dump ice into a bowl full of punch or a pitcher of bloody Marys. It will dilute them irrevocably; both drinks should be poured over a full glass of ice as you would expect at a bar. Try to have the beverage itself already cold from the fridge (or the back doorstep if it's winter) so it won't melt the ice too quickly.

Have lots of neat little square stacks of cocktail napkins in handy spots, or your guests will have handy spots on their clothes and, yes, on your furniture. Don't twist them around in a spiral—it's too June Cleaver.

TOUCH
Having painted myself into this sensory corner, the only thing I can think of that's eminently touchable would be those little linen cocktail napkins that always feel so luxurious, but these should only be considered by rich people who can afford them in the first place and have help in the washing and ironing department. Or by people with no television or books to read who have time to go rooting through old linens in antique shops AND who have the memory available to put the red wine–stained ones in to soak at the end of the party.

TRAYS
Several years ago, Robert Isabell (very smart New York event designer) told me never to mix flowers in with the food. This was such a startling dictum that I am still considering it. I lie awake at night dreaming up arresting configurations of little rocks, sand, peppercorns, herbs, and food on a tray. I often end up using flowers in graphic ways, either a wall-to-wall mat of petals or a little line in a single color down one side, but this is all very "catering" and not usually expected. *Sometimes I think people are lucky to be getting all this delicious food for free, and maybe they should just come into the kitchen and help themselves.*

BEVERAGES
Don't fall into the trap of pre-making vats of a specialty cocktail. I don't know why, but it's inevitable that guests will want whatever ISN'T immediately available. If it's there, they take it to be polite, and then you'll find full glasses on the floor behind the potted plant the next morning, or the potted plant itself will look a little peaky and tell its own tale of abuse.

HORS D'OEUVRES

CURRIED CHICKEN ROLLED IN TOASTED COCONUT
Makes 30 bite-size pieces

I first saw these gorgeous little morsels in the dazzling sunshine of a Caribbean afternoon on the island of Tortola. I had been invited to sail across to another island for dinner, and the owners of the boat, a spirited couple, both in their seventies, had made snacks to sustain us until later. Well, I'm a fool for anything rolled in coconut, and the rather retro combination of chicken, curry, walnuts, and cream cheese totally ruined my dinner. In my excitement—they're awfully good—I ate about twelve, and what with all the bobbing up and down on the water, I started to feel quite queasy. So just eat these in moderation on dry land, and you'll be very happy. An icy Alsace wine like Hugel Gewürztraminer (2001) would be a perfect accessory.

2 cups homemade or College Inn chicken stock

One 8-ounce boneless chicken breast, pounded lightly at the thick end

3 ounces cream cheese, at room temperature

2 tablespoons Homemade Mayonnaise (see recipe, page 53), or Hellmann's mayonnaise

2 tablespoons minced onion

1 teaspoon curry powder

1 cup walnuts, chopped medium-fine

1/2 teaspoon kosher salt

3/4 cup shredded sweetened coconut, toasted on a baking sheet at 350°F for 5 to 7 minutes, or until golden

Put the stock and chicken breast in a small saucepan over low heat. Cover, bring to a simmer, then cook for 8 minutes. Set aside until completely cooled. This could be done the day before. Remove the chicken from the stock (saving the liquid for a soup) and chop medium-fine. In a bowl, beat the cream cheese with the mayonnaise until smooth. Add the chicken, onion, curry powder, walnuts, and salt; mix together gently. Cover the bowl with plastic wrap and refrigerate for a couple of hours—it's much easier to roll when cold. Dampen your hands and lightly roll the mixture into 3/4-inch balls. Press on a coating of toasted coconut and, if you can, serve this hors d'oeuvre within an hour so the coconut will stay crunchy.

SHRIMP TOAST WITH CARAMELIZED PLUM AND GINGER DIP

Makes 40 shrimp toasts

Due to annoying childhood phobias, sadly, I don't eat shellfish. It's not sad for me, just sad for all the people who try to give me something special to eat, like lobster, oysters, or crab. This shrimp toast is the closest I've ever come to conquering my psychological block . . . probably the appeal of the fried bread underneath.

It's easy to summon up a new hors d'oeuvre in the catering company, as we have on hand pretty much any ingredient you can shake a stick at. But, should you go off into the realm of Asian cooking, as in this recipe, it's a good idea to go shopping first and buy the basic ingredients needed if you haven't got them already. You can only improvise so far; for instance, using white wine vinegar instead of rice wine vinegar and fresh ginger instead of pickled will start to weaken pure Asian flavors.

This shrimp toast has to be fried not too long before it's eaten but can be prepared completely ahead of time, even down to the coating of sesame seeds. When you cook it, just keep the door of the kitchen closed, the fan on, and if you're the one doing the cooking, wear a nice big apron. These are delicious enough to warrant having to make them at the last minute.

THE SHRIMP MIXTURE

1 pound fresh shrimp, peeled, deveined, and roughly chopped

2 ounces pickled ginger (see Resources, page 211)

1/4 cup chopped scallions, all the white and a little of the green

1 extra-large egg

1 tablespoon dry sherry

1/2 teaspoon sugar

1 tablespoon cornstarch

1 teaspoon kosher salt

1/2 teaspoon freshly ground black pepper

THE ASSEMBLY

10 slices Pepperidge Farm Very Thin white bread

1 cup sesame seeds

Vegetable oil, for frying

Once you've got everything together the making of the shrimp toast is the definition of quick and easy—just put the shrimp mixture ingredients in a food processor and pulse to form a paste. Spread the mixture on one side of each slice of bread and press facedown onto a plate of sesame seeds. Heat 1/4-inch vegetable oil in a skillet over medium heat. Then fry the toasts for about 2 minutes on both sides, or until golden brown. (If a lot of sesame seeds fall off and start to burn, throw out the oil, wipe the pan, and add fresh oil.) Trim the crusts off and cut each piece into 4 triangles. To serve the shrimp toasts, pass them around, accompanied by the following dip in a small bowl. The shrimp toasts are best hot, so I usually serve them right after they're made.

CARAMELIZED PLUM AND GINGER DIP
Makes one 1 3/4 cups

In an effort to find a fresh and lively sort of plum sauce for the shrimp toasts, I decided to make my own. Not wanting to mess around in the catering kitchen for ages, I just threw everything into one saucepan and asked whoever was standing near the stove to let me know when it became sticky and a bit caramelized.

This sauce has a strong, lip-smacking flavor, which I personally perceived to be totally Asian, but when I handed out little spoonfuls to all the people in my office, they said, "Mmm . . . good barbeque sauce," so now we use it for that too.

1   pound red or black plums, pitted and roughly chopped

1/3 cup dark brown sugar

3   cloves garlic

1/2 cup soy sauce

2   strips orange zest

1/3 cup rice wine vinegar

2 1/2 tablespoons chopped fresh ginger (unpeeled, if the skin is thin)

1/2 teaspoon hot red pepper flakes

Put everything in a small, preferably nonstick saucepan with 1/3 cup water. Cover Ihe pan (this is important), and bring to a simmer. Remove the lid and simmer for about 45 minutes, until there's no liquid on the base of the pan. Put the mixture into the work bowl of a food processor and blend until pretty smooth but with a few little lumps of ginger. Serve in a bowl next to the shrimp toasts.

SALMON GRAVLAX TARTARE ON CRISP POTATO SLICES
Makes about 40 hors d'oeuvres

If you have a nice sharp chef's knife, this is a breeze. (Or if you don't, you should buy a sharpening stone from the resource on page 211, and you'll never have blunt knives again.) The idea for this recipe came about when we were catering a HUGE job on a TINY budget. They wanted tuna tartare, but I knew it would be expensive, and it's best eaten soon after it's made or it starts to get all gummy. Gravlax, on the other hand, needs at least a couple of days to cure, so I decided to use diced salmon instead of tuna, for economy, and to marinate it with our gravlax spice mix a day before the event, freeing up the chefs for other last-minute things. In my test run, I added orange zest, thinking, isn't orange good with salmon?

Normally you would put something like this on a cucumber slice and that would be fine, but the juniper in the marinade suggested potato, so we served it on a slice of crisp

potato, and it was ravishing in the extreme. The potatoes can be made ahead of time too, as long as they're cooked until they're completely crisp and stored in an airtight container until you need them. Any potato not cooked all the way through will soften the others; if that happens, pop them all in a 350°F oven for five minutes, or until they've crisped up again.

The salmon can be sticky, so use two teaspoons to put it on the potato. I could never remember of which there was more in the gravlax cure, sugar or salt (since in the basic gravlax recipe one is three tablespoons and one is four). So after years of irritably looking up such a short recipe, I decided to THINK for a second and realized salt has four letters so salt is the four tablespoons. *Welcome to my world.*

THE GRAVLAX CURE

1 tablespoon juniper berries, chopped

2 teaspoons dried dill

3 tablespoons sugar

4 tablespoons kosher salt (if you only have table salt, 3 tablespoons plus 1 teaspoon would be the correct equivalent)

Mix all the ingredients together in a small bowl. You can make the cure in advance and it will keep, stored in an airtight jar out of the sunlight, for up to 6 months.

THE TARTARE

5 ounces center-cut fresh salmon, skinned, pin-boned, and cut into tiny dice

2 tablespoons Gravlax Cure

1 teaspoon extra-virgin olive oil

1 tablespoon snipped chives

$1/8$ teaspoon grated orange zest

$1/8$ teaspoon freshly ground black pepper

1 bunch dill, minced, for decoration

In a medium bowl, mix the salmon with 2 tablespoons of the Gravlax Cure and then add the olive oil, snipped chives, orange zest, and pepper. Cover and refrigerate overnight, or for at least 6 hours. Serve topped with a scattering of freshly minced dill on a Crisp Potato Slice or an English cucumber slice.

Strew some more minced dill on the plate or tray you're using to pass the hors d'oeuvres—then the Crisp Potato Slices won't skid around and the cucumber will be easier to pick up.

THE CRISP POTATO SLICES
Makes about 40 slices

10 small round potatoes (red or white), cut into $1/8$-inch circular slices (discarding the rounded ends)

$1/2$ cup olive oil

1 teaspoon kosher salt

$1/2$ teaspoon freshly ground black pepper

Position a rack in the top third of the oven and preheat to 350°F.

Arrange the potatoes in a single layer on a baking sheet; brush each slice with oil, then turn them and brush the other side. Sprinkle with salt and pepper and bake for 10 minutes,

THE PASSIONATE SCREW page 91

then turn the slices and bake for another 5 minutes. Remove all the crisp slices with a spatula and continue cooking any slices that look like they need more time. Cool on a rack, then use immediately or store in an airtight container for up to 2 days.

PEPPER-CRUSTED STEAK WITH HORSERADISH CREAM ON CROSTINI

Makes 20 hors d'oeuvres,
with leftovers for delicious sandwiches

I purposefully made this beef marinade super powerful. With this hors d'oeuvre, you only end up with a little mouthful and the peppery flavor needs to come through loud and clear. In the catering company, we shave the beef into small pieces which are then piled onto the crostini, so you can easily bite through without too much effort.

THE BEEF MARINADE

3 cloves garlic, crushed

1/2 teaspoon hot red pepper flakes

1 tablespoon whole black peppercorns, cracked (I fold them in a paper towel and bash them with a hammer)

1 tablespoon minced fresh rosemary leaves

1/3 cup olive oil

2 pounds London broil (top sirloin), cut 1 1/2 inches thick

2 teaspoons kosher salt

Grilled Garlic Crostini (recipe follows)

Horseradish Cream (see recipe, page 54)

Combine the garlic, hot red pepper flakes, peppercorns, rosemary, and olive oil in a Zip-loc bag. Add the beef, coating it with the marinade. Squeeze all the air out of the bag so the beef is enveloped by the marinade, and refrigerate for at least 6 hours, or overnight.

Preheat the grill or broiler for 15 to 20 minutes. Sprinkle the steak with the salt and grill or broil to rare or medium rare, depending on your preference.

The cooking time will depend on the thickness and temperature of the beef, so push at the steak with your finger, and if it still feels totally raw in the middle, give it a little longer. *This is one of the things that cooks just need to intuit and learn to read the silent signs. Better under than overcooked, so check often, and if your finger defeats you, cut the steak with a knife and have a look.* Let the steak rest for at least an hour, to get the juices back into the meat, then cut into short, very thin slices. (The best knife for slicing is a bread knife with wavy rather than pointed teeth, which cuts through beef amazingly well.) Serve on Grilled Garlic Crostini.

GRILLED GARLIC CROSTINI

Makes 15 crostini

1/2 cup olive oil

2 cloves garlic, crushed, or to taste

1 teaspoon kosher salt

1/4 teaspoon freshly ground black pepper

15 1/3-inch slices cut from a French baguette

Italian parsley, minced, for decoration

Mix the olive oil, garlic, salt, and pepper together in a small bowl and brush lightly on both sides of the bread slices. Grill for 15 to 20 seconds on each side, until nicely marked, then remove with tongs and set aside. For broiling, position the rack so the slices are 2 inches from the flame and turn when the crostini starts to blacken at the edges.

Arrange a few shaved slices of beef on each piece of bread, top with a pungent dot of Horseradish Cream (see recipe, page 54), scatter with minced Italian parsley, and dust on a little kosher salt.

HORSERADISH CREAM USES

I love having extra of this cream in the fridge and slathering it on roast beef sandwiches with summer tomatoes and crunchy iceberg lettuce. It's also wonderful mashed into the center of a crisply baked potato. Dust a wet potato with salt and bake at 400°F for 1 hour.

If you have any smoked trout, you can crumble the trout into a little of the cream and pile it on a unpeeled cucumber slice or—stunningly enough—a Wheat Thin.

We discovered this combination when at the catering company we did a party for six hundred of the clotted crème de la crème of New York society. We were sitting around with the client and his minions, trying to decide what on earth to use under the smoked trout that hadn't been done a million times before. One assistant piped up saying his mother used Wheat Thins for everything. Go mom!

KATY'S DATES WITH ANCHO CHILI OIL

Makes 20 or 30 stuffed dates

I first met Katy Sparks in the flesh at New York City's French Culinary Institute. We were both there to teach on a mentorship program, and since I was already wild about the food at her restaurant, Quilty's, I made a beeline for her and insisted we become friends and spend lots of time eating together. For fun, Katy and I have given several cooking classes working as a duet; she made these dates at our first class together. They are just the kind of thing I find irresistible—sweet, crunchy, juicy, spicy—you name it, they've got it. Once you have the ingredients, they're very easy to put together.

THE ANCHO CHILI OIL

1/2 cup extra virgin olive oil

1 tablespoon ancho chili powder (see Resources, page 211)

THE DATES

1/2 cup minced walnuts

1 tablespoon minced fresh sage

2 cloves garlic, minced

1 teaspoon grated orange zest

1 tablespoon olive oil

10 Medjool dates, cut in halves or thirds and pitted

8 thin slices Serrano ham or prosciutto, cut into 3/4-inch-wide strips

RICHARD, JOHN, SERENA, KATY, LAURA, RICHARD, SARAH

To make the ancho chili oil, put the olive oil and the chili powder in a small pan over low heat and warm gently for 10 minutes; set aside for 1 hour to infuse, then strain through a sheet of paper towel. This can be done the day before.

Position a rack at the top of the oven and preheat to 350°F.

In a small bowl, mix the walnuts, sage, garlic, orange zest, and olive oil to form a crumbly paste. Using a teaspoon press the paste into the cavities of the dates. Wrap each date with a 3-inch-long strip of the ham. (The dates can be covered and refrigerated until an hour before guests arrive, when they should be brought to room temperature.)

Place the dates on an ungreased baking sheet and roast for 5 minutes (8, if they're cold); arrange on a serving tray and drip with the ancho chili oil. Serve warm or at room temperature. *Napkins are a must.*

BLACK OR GREEN OLIVADA
Makes 1 cup

If you can find black olives cured in oil (see Note) or cracked green olives with a good flavor, this mixture can be made with either and is wonderful to have on hand all the time. It's perfect on grilled bread or rolled up in warm pita with summer tomatoes. I've swirled a black "comma" in the middle of a white bean soup, anointed olive oil mashed potatoes with the green, and made panini spread with either color topped with shaved Manchego and roasted red peppers (see method for roasted red peppers, page 166).

- 1 cup pitted black olives marinated in oil, or green cracked olives
- 2 strips lemon peel, minced
- 2 tablespoons extra virgin olive oil
- 1 tablespoon minced Italian parsley

Put all the ingredients in the bowl of a food processor and pulse to a grainy paste. Taste for seasoning. Well covered, olivada can be stored in the fridge for up to 3 weeks.

Note: Olives vary enormously; try to find ones that aren't too salty. If you can locate an Italian or Greek specialty shop and taste the olives before buying, that would be your best chance of finding good ones.

PARMESAN, ROSEMARY, AND WALNUT SHORTBREAD
Makes 30 pieces

Crumbly and melting, easy and irresistible, at the catering company, we keep the dough for this shortbread on hand in the freezer for in-house treats and for extra hors d'oeuvres or snacks for a party that balloons at the last minute. Sun-dried Tomato Pesto (recipe follows) on top takes it into sensory overload.

I first tasted this shortbread when my friend Gail Monaghan passed it around in a silver basket before a dinner party at her house. I took one bite and said, "OK, where's the pen? Hand over the recipe (there was a "please" implied): this is amazing and I need to put this in my book." She very angelically wrote it out nicely, and here it is.

8 tablespoons (1 stick) unsalted butter, at room temperature

4 ounces freshly grated Parmesan cheese

1 cup Heckers or King Arthur all-purpose flour

1 tablespoon minced fresh rosemary

1/2 cup walnuts, toasted at 350°F for 10 minutes, then chopped

1/2 teaspoon kosher salt

1/4 teaspoon freshly ground black pepper

Pinch cayenne pepper

Using an electric mixer, cream the butter; add the Parmesan, and mix well. Stir in the flour, rosemary, walnuts, salt, black pepper, and cayenne. Form the mixture into 1-inch-wide logs, wrap them in plastic, and refrigerate for at least half an hour, or up to 3 days.

When you're ready to bake the shortbread, position a rack in the middle of the oven and preheat to 350°F. Line a baking sheet with parchment. Cut the logs into 1/4-inch-thick slices, place the slices on the baking sheet, and bake for 20 minutes, or until golden at the edges. Remove the shortbread slices and cool them on a wire rack. You can offer these by themselves passed in a basket, or top them with the Sun-dried Tomato Pesto.

Note: Buy the absolutely best Parmesan (preferably Reggiano) you can find. Ideally, get a lump and grate it yourself. Look for a chunk with rind on only one side, not two.

SUN-DRIED TOMATO PESTO
Makes 1 cup

1 cup sun-dried tomatoes in oil, drained and chopped

2 tablespoons sun-dried tomato oil or olive oil

6 fresh sage leaves

1 to 2 garlic cloves, to taste

Put all the ingredients in the bowl of a food processor and blend to a paste. Use 1/2 teaspoonful on each shortbread.

COCKTAILS

I used to own a bar called "Serena" and was partners with my son Sam. He took care of the business and his finger-on-the-nightlife-pulse side of things, and I wandered around talking to strangers and picking up cigarette butts. I never got used to the idea that people would stub their cigarettes out on the floor; what were people thinking? I felt the bar was an extension of my living room at home—especially with Patrick McMullan's fabulous 80's photographic portraits on the walls.

We had a spectacular four years, then sold at just the right moment. I had the greatest fun inventing new cocktails using Sam and his friends as guinea pigs. The friends' eyes would roll in delight, and they all demanded just ONE more drink—to be absolutely sure it was good. They were so helpful.

THE PASSIONATE SCREW

(see photograph, page 84)

The Passionate Screw (in my mind, naturally evolved from a screwdriver, since it had passion fruit in) was the most popular. Women sidled up to the good-looking bartenders to ask nicely for a Passionate Screw, and men had the pleasure of snapping their fingers (yes) at the beautiful waitresses and demanding one.

1 1/2 ounces Absolut Kurant

1 ounce passion fruit puree (see Note 2, page 94 and Resources, page 211)

1 ounce cranberry juice

Lemon twist, for garnish

Add the ingredients to a shaker half filled with ice, shake well, and strain into a double rocks glass over ice.

THE PINK BITCH

THE SMART BLOND

CLICQUOT RICO

BRIAN'S TKO PUNCH

THE PINK BITCH

The Pink Bitch came about when I redecorated while we were closed down—that's another story—just before 9/11. We reopened three months later, surrounded by the fuchsia glow of Ralph Lauren's Aruba Pink paint. The bar looked amazing and we needed a cocktail for the reopening party. It had to be pink without being girly so (in my mind, naturally evolved from a Pink Lady) Pink Bitch it was.

1 1/2   ounces Absolut Citron

1/2   ounce raspberry puree (see Note 1, page 94)

1/2   ounce fresh lemon juice

Splash of Sprite

Lemon wedge, for garnish

Add all the ingredients to a shaker half filled with ice. Shake well and strain into a double rocks glass over ice.

CLICQUOT RICO

Happily, we found that the only word which rhymes with Clicquot was a tasty white rum.

1 1/2   ounces Ron Rico rum

1 1/2   ounces pineapple juice

2   ounces Veuve Clicquot Champagne

Fresh Pineapple wedge, for garnish

Add the ingredients to a Champagne glass, in the order listed.

THE SMART BLOND

Smart Blond was simply a late night mix-fest prompted by the thought, "If I see another green apple martini, I shall positively scream . . . let's make a nice yellow drink," so I did.

1 1/2   ounces Absolut Citron

1/2   ounce peach schnapps

1   ounce passion fruit puree (see Note 2, page 94 and Resources, page 211)

Squeeze of fresh lime juice

Sprig ot fresh mint, for garnish

Add all the ingredients to a shaker half filled with ice. Shake well, strain into a martini glass.

BRIAN'S TKO PUNCH

My friend Brian Gracie's TKO Punch is rather depressing—where's the hammock? Where's the Caribbean??—until you drink it, and suddenly nothing matters and you can hear turquoise waves breaking, wherever you are, even in your own living room.

3   ounces fresh orange juice

1   ounce Bacardi rum

1/2   ounce crème de banana

1/2   ounce blackberry brandy

Slice of orange, for garnish

Add all the ingredients to a shaker half filled with ice. Shake well and pour into a tall glass.

THE ROPE BURN

For a long time we had *Tex in the City* nights at the bar, once a month. This little drink got everybody extremely relaxed and happy to sing, dance, and bid on raffle tickets while wearing great big hats. No, they weren't blind-drunk, just relaxed.

1 $^1/_2$ ounces Cuervo Gold tequila

$^1/_2$ ounce fresh lime juice

2   teaspoons sugar

Splash of Tabasco, to taste

Wedge of lime, for garnish

Add the ingredients to a shaker half filled with ice, shake well, and strain into a shot glass.

PIMM'S CUP

Pimm's came to light around 1840. This 50 proof drink might sound and look—awash as it is, with citrus, cucumber, and mint—rather lightweight; but it packs a wallop and has contributed to many a romantic misdemeanor in the English shires.

Unless you have a fast-drinking crowd, don't make too much at once, as it's nice to keep the ginger ale sparkling.

2   ounces Pimm's No.1

2   ounces Tanqueray gin

6   ounces ginger ale

THE ROPE BURN

Slices of orange and lemon

Cucumber peel

Sprigs of fresh mint

Keep the Pimm's, gin, and ginger ale well chilled. Mix everything together and serve over ice, with some fruit, cucumber, and mint in each glass. Multiply the ingredients proportionately if you want to fill a punch bowl or a pitcher.

Note 1: For the raspberry puree, add $^1/_3$ to $^1/_2$ cup sugar to 2 packed cups, fresh or frozen raspberries, depending on sweetness.

Note 2: To sweeten the frozen passion fruit juice, add $^1/_2$ cup sugar to 1 cup juice.

ALL DRINK RECIPES ARE FOR ONE SERVING.

LET ME HELP YOU HELP THEM

In this chapter, I have chosen Italy, England, and America, three countries with very distinctive food. In planning a buffet, this is the easiest way to present food with a focus that everyone can relate to, and it avoids a buffet table with a potluck look.

Each country's section starts with six design ideas (incorporating food, platters, and flowers) that capture the country's character and make it simple to emulate—they might even get you a reputation as a theatrical wizard. Alternatively, you can just use the recipes and put it all out on the kitchen table, and no doubt, people will be perfectly delighted.

Look, for example, at the beginning of the American section (page 144). You'll find "Speaking American," with tips, which if followed would say loud and clear "this is an All-American buffet," as much as if you had "America the Beautiful" drifting out from a tape recorder under the table. On the opposite page, you can see how it comes together in a drawing of fried chicken, cornbread, succotash, and other indigenous food. You'll see a table covered in blue-and-white striped linen, anchored by big bunches of red lilies and gerberas in tall glass vases—it's a glamorous look designed to enhance simple, familiar food.

Before you actually get to the recipes, I have given an overview, which includes how to design the table, how to choose the right platter for the right food, and how to help the guests get at the food in an organized manner and then . . . move them right along (so the people at the back of the line can get a look in). Having someone to help is ideal so you aren't worn to a frazzle before the end of the meal and never get to eat a bite of your own wonderful food.

Most people are so happy to have finished cooking the food that to start delving ever deeper into the whys and wherefores of a buffet would be altogether too much for them to tolerate. *They must be saluted for their good efforts and allowed to go and have a bubble bath.*

Here are some things that you might want to think about:

THE TABLE

I have seen buffet tables as flat as the sliced deli meats that were on them. I also once saw a table exhibiting a veritable countryside of plants and flowers. Huge platters of food were balanced on faux-wooden logs, and something that looked like a little pond with a ladle was actually the sauce for the fish. The whole thing was useful as a conversation piece, but the stuffed fox(!) bang in the middle was a bit spooky. Ideally, your buffet will fall somewhere between these two.

Concerning the cloth, better to drape it on the floor than have it hanging at half-mast—unless you're in the garden, with reams of muslin and a playful breeze so the cloth can billow at will. If the table is positioned against a wall, just pull the cloth down at the front—the back doesn't matter, as no one will see, and it will give you extra room underneath for storing clutter.

ERGONOMICS

If you can position the buffet table so it goes with the flow of the evening and you're lucky enough to have an overhead light on a dimmer, put the table under that. It's nice if a little light can shine down directly on the table since flickering votives, which are basically on the same level as the food, and candles in candlesticks don't shed enough light for your guests to either appreciate the beautiful food or to choose their favorite things. Ideally, position the table as close to the kitchen as

possible and out of the way of the bar or the drinks area, which is usually a human logjam.

Look at the flow of the room and decide which way would be best for your guests to move through the buffet. Put the plates at the beginning side of the table, and when they've got their food . . . encourage your guests to move AWAAAYY from the buffet by positioning everyone's knives and forks—rolled in a napkin, or laid in a basket—on another table a few feet farther on from the food.

I usually put a basket of interesting breads or rolls on that table too, but if it's garlic bread, make sure the slices are cut all the way through. It's so annoying to pick up a slice of bread and have the rest of the loaf hanging by its underneath crust, which has turned into steel and won't separate from the piece you're trying to pick up (with one hand) no matter how hard you shake it.

If you don't plan to seat everyone around a table, try to make the food easy to eat with just a fork. Cut chicken breasts into slices and avoid anything on the bone. Most people don't mind perching on the arm of a sofa or sitting on the stairs to eat, but having to use a knife to saw through food, with a plate wobbling on their knees, is too much to ask and asking for trouble.

MYSTERY FOOD

Out of respect for the people at the back of the line, avoid food that's not easily identifiable. It will become that dreaded "mystery" food (see below) that causes people to stop in their tracks and prompts frowns and whispered questions among your guests. If you don't want to stand on guard ready to explain what the fiddlehead fern risotto is, save it for a small dinner party, since if something looks suspect, you're bound to hear . . .

"Does this have any . . ."

"cilantro?"

"garlic?"

"nuts?"

"dangerously hot chiles? "

COLORS

I prefer to use all white, glass, or silver platters and to let the food and flowers provide the colors on the table. Make a list of what you're serving and note the color of each food—you'll find they're mostly green, brown, red, orange, and white with handy bits of pink and yellow. Well—however eccentric you are—you can't have five red things all on the left of the table, so juggle the platters and spread the red judiciously.

You might want to lay salmon fillets on a bed of dazzling orange carrots to make a statement, or you might want to put the carrots on the other side of the table for a splash of color next to a green salad. If you have a fine meal, but in possibly drab colors (brown, brown, beige, and dark green), try to introduce color in orange glass votive holders, a pyramid of lemons, or a stack of cobalt blue linen napkins. I'm always amazed at the things I have lying around that, with a splash of inspiration, can be roped into service.

Flowers can set the scene in an instant. They add big blocks of color and, just as importantly, height. I have already mentioned red lilies, which I feel are exuberantly American; Italy makes me think of grapevines or, more elegantly, evergreen topiary; and England is all about garden roses, lavender, and trailing ivy.

SHAPES

Even though I have a pretty good idea of the platters and bowls I own, I admit to having forgotten about twenty percent of them, which is actually fine, as it affords me great delight—rediscovering old favorites buried under the newer stuff.

When you're out in antique or kitchen shops, keep your eyes open for interesting dishes, bearing in mind that which you already possess. Look for square, rectangular, or oval

shapes, or anything unusual, and then when you need a particular dish, chances are you'll have it. I sometimes find beautiful antiques knocked down to a pittance because of a large chip on the edge, which could be hidden with a hefty sprig of herbs and no one would know the difference. There are endless possibilities, and eventually you'll collect a lot of dishes in useful shapes and sizes that will serve you well—whatever you're serving.

Good utensils are vital—remember, your guests are holding a plate and have one hand left with which to pick up the food. Tongs are great. I have found ones with spoonlike ends and also ones with a flat side and a curved fork side, which are perfect for fish or sliced tomatoes and mozzarella. Short-handled spoons with a fairly large capacity are good, but make

sure they are proportionate to the bowl they're destined for and not so short that they fall in and get covered in sauce or olive oil.

If you have food with a mind of its own and no tongs, providing bowls and platters with straight sides will give your guests something to capture the food against using just a spoon (without winging buttery new potatoes straight across the room). Try to find a nice salad spoon and fork that are hinged in the middle (with room in the handles for actual human fingers), as most people will stop and put their plates down to maneuver individual spoons and forks—and stopping is what you want to avoid.

If you have more than twelve people, you might want to have both a main platter or bowl and a smaller one in reserve in the

kitchen to swap out when the food in the first one is looking demolished. I often think that when all the food is out at the same time it looks more like army rations than a delicious home-cooked meal. In the bad old days, I would put out a platter for twenty people of, for instance, sliced, grilled chicken breast interspersed with herbs and lemon wedges. All very well and beautiful for about TWO MINUTES, until my ebullient friends inevitably took some from every corner, causing the whole thing to look like a big mess. Order was restored by putting the chicken breasts in a row on a long narrow platter, so only the most delinquent guest would do anything other than take the next piece in line.

HELP

And when I say "help" I don't necessarily mean a fleet of tuxedoed professionals (though they have their place). If you have lots of people over for dinner, it will be much more fun for you if you have some backup. In the past, when I deemed the number of guests was about to become out of hand, I often requisitioned my teenage children's friends, who usually astonished me with their competence. So try to find someone to monitor the kitchen and, if you can wangle it, someone to be out among the guests too, clearing the plates away, mopping up spills, and generally being indispensable. Without a little help, I am incapable of sitting sociably with my guests, since when something needs doing, I go straight into my headwaiter/busboy role, which, once entered into, usually lasts for the rest of the night and makes everyone very nervous.

ITALIAN BUFFET

Classic Pork Roast Rolled with
Fontina and Prosciutto

Tonno alla Griglia con Fagioli e Gremolata
(Grilled Tuna with Cannellini Beans)

Pasta, Peppers, and Pignoli

Roasted Eggplant, Fresh Tomato,
and Basil Salad

Arugula with Sautéed Artichoke Hearts

Kim's Tomato-Shallot Vinaigrette

Roast Cauliflower with Raisins and Thyme

Garlic Bread with Green Herb Butter

Venetian Pears

Free-form Plum, Rosemary,
and Orange Crostata

A TUSCAN HOLIDAY STORY My sister and I had been talking about a holiday in Italy for over a year. We both have businesses that consume our lives, and timing was the big problem. The only month we had free was August, which, as Europeans will tell you, is hell on wheels. Every good restaurant is closed, it's boiling hot, and you're more than likely to see at least two people who live on your very own street sitting on the steps of a church, shading their heads with a map or a guidebook. My trusty sister found what sounded like an enchanting farmhouse in Tuscany with a separate guest area, but we remembered the last place we found that sounded charming was Villa Jasmine on the Greek island of Paxos, which had saltwater running out of the showers in the bathroom. Our Italian farmhouse boasted a swimming pool, so we stepped into the void and signed up for three weeks.

The trip there was problematic. Delayed flights, lost luggage, the wrong rental car, and then my inability to read a map. Notwithstanding these hurdles, we turned down a narrow dirt road leading to La Columbaia a little past midnight. We enjoyed a minute of self-congratulation as we bumped along, until our headlights illuminated a modern brick building with a space under it occupied by a new tractor and an old Fiat. There was a covered structure opposite sheltering four other cars and three motorbikes.

A scruffy blond dog shot out of his kennel and started barking his head off.

This was not idyllic or even particularly bucolic. We sat in a bark-punctuated silence . . . I, determined not to say a single word, my sister gathering her spirits. The house was worse inside. We are both horrible snobs concerning interior decoration and this was our come-uppance. The last words my good sister said as we trudged into our bedrooms were, "I'm sure it'll all look better in the morning."

I awoke at seven A.M. The skimpy curtains had been closed the night before, and now they had a halo of golden light around them. I twitched the printed cotton aside with some trepidation. The panorama from my little window was the exquisite Tuscany of the Renaissance (very familiar from my art history classes) with smooth rolling hills, perfectly positioned cypress trees, and a trailing mesh of grapevines. In the distance, a farmer and his dog were already out inspecting the grapes.

Our host's farmhouse was pale pink stucco with a white dovecote perched on one end and a wooden pergola woven through with wisteria that gave shade to a wide, flagstone terrace. What great timeless beauty unfolded before me. This ancient picture could only have been improved to my heathen eye—as it in fact was—by a dazzling swimming pool just below the terrace. I felt sorry for the people in the pink farmhouse, as they had to look at us.

I opened the front door to inspect further and nearly fell over a big "Treasures of Tuscany" welcome basket that had been left on our step by the owners. It contained a bottle of moss-green olive oil, a bottle of red wine vinegar stuffed with thyme, and a bunch of muscat grapes with untouched bloom and curled tendrils springing from the stalk. A fat wasp crawled over one of four golden plums; there were radiant tomatoes and a sheaf of small-leaved basil. Manhattan was a world away—this was not the farmers' market . . . this was the farm.

At that very moment, an elegant woman came round the corner carrying the only things missing for breakfast—speckled brown eggs and a big, crusty loaf. I managed to get out a "Molto grazie" and "che bella campagna," but with a smile she was gone.

Because I am the youngest one, I love surprising this particular sister with my competence. I opened her bedroom door and said, "Buongiorno, cara. Breakfast in ten minutes."

We reveled in the pure flavors of our first Tuscan meal—eggs fried in olive oil and mopped up with thickly sliced bread that I'd grilled and then rubbed with tomatoes. We picked the little basil leaves off the stems and ate them one by one till our mouths grew numb, then we happily started in on the grapes and spat the pits out of the window in a rustic manner.

The big blond dog wandered in, shook himself violently, and flopped down, settling his chin on my foot. He—just as much as we—suddenly felt very much at home.

SPEAKING ITALIAN

A hunk of the best Parmesan you can find, with a little wooden handled dagger of a cheese knife stabbed into it so people can help themselves

Grissini breadsticks

Wrought-iron candelabra with spikes to hold pillar candles—a Mexican candelabra would look fine

A pair of rosemary topiaries in terra cotta, stone, or classical metal containers flanking the table

A shallow bowl of cold-pressed olive oil perfumed with thyme threads, garlic shavings, and a strip of lemon zest, for dressing the salad

A small glass carafe of aged balsamic vinegar or Vincotto, also for the salad

CLASSIC PORK ROAST ROLLED WITH FONTINA AND PROSCIUTTO

Serves 10

I wrote the word "classic" just so you know I do know there's nothing revolutionary about this recipe—unless you haven't tasted it before, then it will effectively astound you. The flavors are impeccably balanced, surprising but familiar, like a memory from a past life, when you were a gondolier in Venice or a principessa in Padua. Each component of the dish should be perfect in itself, starting with a good piece of meat from a reliable butcher, then the best prosciutto, imported Fontina cheese, and fresh sage leaves.

Cutting into the loin to create a flat piece of meat takes a moment's consideration, but just do it slowly and you'll be fine. Ask the butcher to give you some of his string so you can tie up the meat after you've rolled it back into shape.

- 4 pounds pork loin, trimmed of excess fat

- 1 tablespoon kosher salt, or to taste

- 1 teaspoon freshly ground black pepper, or to taste

- 12 fresh sage leaves, washed and dried, stalks trimmed, plus 1 bunch perfect fresh sage, for decoration

- Six 1/8-inch-thick slices Fontina cheese

- 5 thin slices prosciutto di Parma

- 2 tablespoons golden olive oil, such as Filippo Berio brand

Cut into the loin in a short spiral (see illustration below) and then lay the meat out flat. Scatter it with a little salt and pepper, then polka dot on the sage leaves. Put 4 slices of cheese down next, then lay on the prosciutto to cover the cheese. Grind on some black pepper, then another couple of slices of cheese for good measure. Now re-roll the meat into its original, but fatter, shape. You'll find it's easier to roll it away from you rather than sideways or toward you. Position the rolled meat so the seam is on the bottom and tie the roll in 5 or 6 places with butcher's string, tight enough to make a compact shape but not so tight that the string cuts into the meat. It's easiest if you tie about an inch in from each end first to secure the whole thing, then tie the middle. If you have time, prepare this the day before and hold overnight, well covered with plastic wrap in the fridge. It gets the preparation out of the way and gives the flavors a chance to integrate.

Position a rack in the upper third of the oven and preheat to 350°F. Weigh the rolled loin.

Heat a large, preferably nonstick saucepan with the oil over high heat, sprinkle more salt over the meat, and sear on all sides to a deep golden brown. It's harder to reach into a high-sided pan, but it certainly makes cleanup easier. Put the pork on a sheet pan and roast for 12 minutes per pound of total weight, or until a meat thermometer reads 145°F. When

it comes out of the oven, loosen any cheese that has oozed out and crusted onto the pan. The roast pork must rest for 20 to 30 minutes before you remove the string and slice the meat 1/3 inch thick—any thinner and it will fall apart—or the roast can be held for a couple of hours and served at room temperature. Serve on a platter with a bunch of sage. If there are leftovers, they make a wonderful sandwich on focaccia with garlicky mayonnaise and some peppery arugula leaves.

TONNO ALLA GRIGLIA CON FAGIOLI E GREMOLATA (GRILLED TUNA WITH CANNELLINI BEANS)
Serves 12

This dish, more than almost any other, reminds me of Italy. Not because I had it in Italy necessarily, but because it was my favorite thing to eat at Meridiana, a long-departed, hip Italian restaurant on London's Fulham Road. I was quite young and impressionable and had never imagined such a combination as fish and beans. (Pasta with garlic and broccoli rabe was wildly foreign enough for me.)

Then, one evening at the restaurant, there was a new waiter, Sergio, lounging by the desserts, arranging his hair in a distant mirror. I was mesmerized by him, and would have agreed with anything that came out of his mouth, so when this Adonis waxed on about the Tonno e Fagioli, naturally I ordered them.

When his tanned hand placed an azure plate with pearly beans and pink fish, strewn with shards of purple onion and glistening, green Italian parsley, in front of me . . . well, like the fish, I was hooked.

This simple Italian dish made me feel very sophisticated, and with every visit I would concur with the smiling Italians that, yes indeed, signorina would **ADORE** the Tonno e Fagioli (and sotto voce) . . . "con Sergio."

Nowadays, I grill fresh tuna—it's much more interesting than the original, which was, in all its deliciousness, out of a can. You could serve this tuna rare (à la Nobu), but I prefer it medium. You can arrange it on the beans when it's still warm or hold it for a couple of hours sitting in its juices. Both ways are good; just don't refrigerate the cooked fish before arranging it on the beans, or it will become too firm. If you have leftovers, obviously you'll have to refrigerate them, but the next day you can slice the now firm tuna for a sandwich with tomatoes and olivada (see recipe, page 89) on crusty Tuscan bread.

THE TUNA

1 1/2   cups extra virgin olive oil

2   tablespoons minced lemon zest

2   tablespoons minced garlic

2   tablespoons minced fresh rosemary leaves

1   teaspoon hot red pepper flakes

6   teaspoons kosher salt, divided

4   pounds center-cut tuna, trimmed of skin and dark tissue cut into 1-inch-thick slices

1/4   cup fresh lemon juice

1   red onion, sliced (reserve for assembly)

1   bunch Italian parsley, for decoration

To make the marinade, mix the olive oil, lemon zest, garlic, rosemary, pepper flakes, and 2 teaspoons of the salt together in large bowl, and set aside.

Cut the tuna slices into 12 equal portions, then toss with the marinade and arrange the pieces side by side in a flat, nonreactive dish big enough to hold the marinade and all the tuna in one layer. Cover with plastic and refrigerate for at least 2 hours, or overnight. Take the steaks out of the refrigerator 1 hour before cooking and turn them over. Get the grill or broiler red hot (allow 30 minutes); sprinkle both sides of the steaks with 4 teaspoons of the salt and cook the fish the way you prefer, from rare to well-done, 2 to 4 minutes per side. Transfer from the heat to the serving platter and let cool for 10 minutes. Pour the lemon juice over the steaks while they're still warm.

THE BEANS

This may not seem like a lot of beans for twelve people, but it is part of a buffet and there will be other dishes to choose from, so I think it is enough. If you serve this by itself, increase the quantities.

1 1/2   pounds dried cannellini beans

2   bay leaves

4   large cloves garlic

2   tablespoons plus 1/2 teaspoon kosher salt

1/4   cup extra virgin olive oil

1/2   teaspoon freshly ground black pepper

1/3   cup minced Italian parsley leaves

Put the beans in a large pan, cover with 6 inches of cold water, and set aside to soak overnight. The next day, drain the beans and put them back in the pan with the bay leaves and garlic. Cover with 4 inches of water and bring to a simmer over medium heat (see Note). Cook until al dente, 60 to 70 minutes, then add 2 tablespoons of the salt and cook another 5 minutes or so, until tender. Drain, reserving 1/4 cup of the cooking liquid, then tip the beans and the 1/4 cup liquid onto a sheet pan to cool for 15 minutes, removing the garlic and bay leaves or not. Toss the beans in a large bowl with the olive oil and 1/2 teaspoon each of the salt and pepper. When the beans have cooled, fold in the parsley and set aside.

Note: Simmering the beans instead of boiling them and using a big pan with lots of water, cooks them more evenly and stops them from breaking up. Don't hold back on the salt, or you'll hardly taste any salt at all.

THE GREMOLATA

If you try this on its own, it's quite overpowering. Don't worry—once scattered over the whole dish, it will be perfect. Don't grate the zest: Remove it with a potato peeler and mince with a sharp knife.

- 1/2 cup minced Italian parsley leaves and a few crunchy stems
- 3 strips lemon zest, minced
- 2 strips orange zest, minced
- 3 garlic cloves, minced
- 1 teaspoon kosher salt

In a small bowl, toss together the parsley, lemon zest, orange zest, garlic, and salt.

To serve the Tonno alla Griglia con Fagioli e Gremolata, make a hill of beans (not often you can say that) on a shallow platter and arrange the tuna steaks on top, reserving the accumulated juices. Just before the guests arrive, pour the juices over the fish, scatter with the red onions, then the gremolata. For decoration, stuff a vivacious (i.e., full of life) bunch of parsley in at one end of the platter.

PASTA, PEPPERS, AND PIGNOLI
Serves 10

This is incredibly easy, elegant peasant food. It's the Sophia Loren of pasta dishes, heady with garlic, sensuous and desirable but with excellent posture and very fine cheekbones.

Farfalle is a perfect pasta to use for a buffet, as it's pretty, and easy to stab with just a fork. If you can find heavy, firm Holland peppers they're the best choice; the flesh is sweet and dense so when it's cooked it still has some bite. Fresh oregano has a wonderful tangy taste but dried is fine.

- 5 Holland red peppers
- 1/4 cup extra virgin olive oil
- 2 cloves garlic, crushed
- 2 tablespoons chopped fresh oregano (or 2 teaspoons dried), plus the rest of the fresh bunch for decoration

$^1/_4$ cup plus 1 teaspoon kosher salt

$^3/_4$ teaspoon freshly ground black pepper

1 pound farfalle pasta

$^1/_3$ cup pignoli (pine nuts)

Preheat the broiler for 15 minutes.

Stand each pepper on its base and slice the flesh down in four vertical slabs and then lay skin-side up on a foil lined baking sheet. Remove each slice as it's nicely blackened, put in a Ziploc bag and set aside to steam.

In a medium bowl, mix together the olive oil, garlic, oregano, 1 teaspoon of kosher salt, and the black pepper, and set aside. When the peppers have cooled, peel them and slice across into $^1/_4$-inch-wide ribbons. Toss the peppers with the olive oil mixture and either set aside for about an hour or put in a plastic container and refrigerate overnight.

Bring a large saucepan of water to a boil; add the $^1/_4$ cup salt and the pasta. Return to a slow boil, stir a couple of times and cook until al dente, about 12 minutes, depending on the brand of pasta.

Drain, and if you can tip the pasta out onto a sheet pan to cool, do that. If you will be tipping it into a bowl, I would (against all form) run the pasta briefly under cold water to stop the cooking, as the heat won't dissipate in a bowl and the pasta could continue to cook.

Mix the peppers with the pasta and the pine nuts. Just before serving, if you used the fresh oregano, scatter sprigs of the herb over the dish for decoration.

ROASTED EGGPLANT, FRESH TOMATO, AND BASIL SALAD
Serves 10

I prefer to use Japanese or Italian eggplant for this dish (see Note 1). Both are almost seedless, with less chance of bitterness and a good inside-to-outside ratio. This is a wonderful mixture and can be used as a rustic hors d'oeuvre on grilled bread or spooned on top of a breaded chicken cutlet, hot from the pan, to perk up a simple dinner. In the catering kitchen we've tossed it with farfalle for a pasta salad and made sandwiches, layering it with smoked turkey. The recipe was first published in *New York* magazine in May 2001, and if ONE MORE PERSON tells me how much they just love it, and use it all the time . . . I guess I would be very pleased.

3 pounds Japanese or Italian eggplant

1 tablespoon kosher salt

1 teaspoon freshly ground black pepper

3/4 cup extra virgin olive oil

1 1/2 pounds firm but ripe plum tomatoes or tomatoes on the vine

3/4 cup loosely packed basil leaves

2 garlic cloves, minced

3 tablespoons aged sherry vinegar (see Resources, page 211)

Position a rack at the top of the oven and preheat to 400°F.

Cut the stalk end off the eggplants and peel a wide stripe down each side with a vegetable peeler. Cut the eggplants into 1-inch diagonal chunks and put them on a sheet pan. If the eggplants are more than 2 inches thick, slice the thick ends in half lengthwise before cutting into chunks. Toss with the salt and pepper and then drizzle with the olive oil (see Note 2). Roast for 35 to 45 minutes, turning carefully a couple of times with a metal spatula.

While the eggplant is roasting, trim the stalk ends off the tomatoes. Cut the tomatoes in half vertically, then lay each half flat on a cutting board. Make 2 or 3 cuts (depending on the size of the tomato) in one direction, then angling your knife to 45 degrees, make 2 or 3 cuts crosswise, in an aim to create 3/4-inch diagonal cubes.

After 35 to 45 minutes, poke at the eggplant with your finger and make sure it's nice and crisply caramelized on the outside and squishy on the inside. If any of the larger pieces are at all hard or have an opaque look to them, allow another 5 minutes and test again, as undercooked eggplant is quite terrible. *(Despite some people's wish for absolutes, there has to come a time when the cook's own eye and good judgment take over.)* Remove from the oven, give a final turn with the spatula, and set aside on the pan to cool.

When you're ready to assemble the salad, pull the basil leaves into small pieces and toss with the tomatoes and garlic in a large bowl; stir in the sherry vinegar, then carefully fold in the cooled eggplant. Check for taste and decide whether you need more salt, pepper, or olive oil. Serve this salad at room temperature on the same day it's made. It's still good after refrigeration, but the tomato flavor will suffer from the cold.

Note 1: If you use regular eggplant, cut into cubes and toss them with 3 tablespoons kosher salt. Tip the cubes into a strainer set over a bowl; put a plate in the strainer resting on the cubes, and place anything that weighs about 3 pounds on the plate. Leave for 30 minutes. Pat the eggplant dry with paper towels and continue as above.

Note 2: When you pour the oil over the eggplant, toss it through immediately or it will instantly get soaked up and you won't have enough olive oil left to coat all the pieces.

ARUGULA WITH SAUTÉED ARTICHOKE HEARTS
Serves 10

Perfect arugula is not always easy to find. The leaves bruise if mishandled and can become too peppery and almost acrid when old. When searching for arugula that can stand on its own, I always ask the produce vendor if I can taste a leaf from a bunch that's for sale. They have yet to say no, which is lucky, as tasting is the only way to tell if you have found a good batch.

If you're not going to use the arugula immediately, trim the stems at the base and wrap the arugula loosely but airtight in aluminum foil. When I was catering from North Salem in Westchester, I hired the most wonderful young woman called Amarilis. She was from Guatemala, and it was her habit to wrap all our herbs in this way to keep them fresh. I was astonished at the efficacy of her technique, but she just gave me one of her pitying, "What else you do?" looks, so I didn't go on about it too much.

In the catering company, we use the hearts of large fresh artichokes, poach them in homemade chicken stock until al dente, cut them in wedges, and sauté in half butter and half olive oil, adding fresh tarragon at the last minute. They're really amazing and everyone adores them. If you can find frozen artichoke hearts, you could follow the same procedure, as it's much quicker and easier, but don't use the marinated ones in a jar; they're too vinegary.

6 large artichokes

2 lemons, cut in half equatorially

1 quart chicken stock (homemade or College Inn)

1/4 cup golden olive oil

2 tablespoons unsalted butter

2 tablespoons chopped fresh tarragon leaves (or 1 tablespoon dried)

12 ounces arugula leaves (about 4 bunches, trimmed)

Look for firm, tight artichokes and choose the heavier ones. Cut the leaves off two-thirds of the way down from the top; snap off all the remaining leaves and scrape out the hairy choke with a sharp-edged spoon. Trim around each artichoke heart to make it neat and rub with the cut lemon to prevent discoloration. Put the hearts and the chicken stock in a medium saucepan over medium heat and simmer until al dente, 10 to 20 minutes. Drain, reserving the stock for a vegetable soup, and when the artichoke hearts have cooled enough to handle, cut each one into 8 wedges. Put a shallow pan over high heat, add the olive oil and butter, and when they're hot, sauté the wedges until golden brown, 5 or 6 minutes, adding the tarragon just before they're ready. Set the sautéed artichokes aside to cool a bit. Wash the arugula well, twice if need be, as it can be relentlessly gritty, spin dry, and put it in a wide salad bowl, scatter the warm hearts on top, and either toss together with Kim's Tomato-Shallot Vinaigrette (recipe follows) or serve the vinaigrette in a bowl on the side.

KIM'S VINAIGRETTE STORY When I lived in North Salem, on February 5, 1993, at 8:45 in the evening, Kim turned up at my front door. It seemed every woman of a certain age in Westchester had heard of Kim. The word was, he was *an intense, moody, single artist with a misty past and big blue eyes.* He was the last person to arrive at a dinner I was giving and came to join a friend of mine—but just as a friend, she insisted.

I went to the door to let him in and encountered, literally, the most attractive man I'd ever seen. The "big blue eyes" rumor was partially true—they were not huge, but lapis blue and dancing over high flushed cheekbones and a smiling mouth. It was silently snowing, and against the weather he wore a Norwegian army pillbox hat (at a very rakish angle for a straight man) and was bundled into a big black coat with an upturned collar. I didn't know at the time that he was well aware of the effect he had—I was just affected.

I paused and said calmly (as the mind did a pirouette) . . ."You must be Kim," and then as I closed the door, "Come and be introduced." He moved forward and I trailed after him like a baby chick following a shiny red wagon.

We joined the others. "I think there's a chair over there, " I said, pointing, ". . . next to me, actually." My darling, helpful friend Ann asked if there was anything she could do. I said absently, "Yes, just get everything on the table and let us know when it's ready." I had abandoned the meal and was now busy—sitting next to Kim.

It was an Indian meal, complex and impressive. The next morning, Kim called and said it had been so good, he really wished he could have taken his plate into another room so he could REALLY concentrate on all

the different textures and flavors. Well (I decided), that was sex talk if ever I'd heard it. *Take it into another room indeed . . . the BEDROOM, maybe.*

A few days later I called and invited him for dinner, planning to impress him with succotash and apple pie. I was QUITE nervous. Since he'd mentioned that he liked to cook too, when he arrived, I asked him if he could possibly make a vinaigrette for our salad.

He rolled up his sleeves; his forearms were fascinating, all muscles, sinews, and smooth skin. I loved the way he sharpened the knife on the stone—dexterous to a fault. I loved the way he smacked the garlic clove with the blade and flicked away the papery skin with the tip. The garlic, with a big pinch of fleur de sel, was reduced to a puree in seconds. Kim minced a shallot, minced a plum tomato, and slid everything off the board into a bowl. With one hand, he squeezed the juice from half a lemon (forearm rippling nicely) and then, with his thumb controlling the flow, sprinkled on aged sherry vinegar. He loosened the silver knob on the pepper grinder and ground a rough shower of black pepper. Extra virgin olive oil was chosen and whisked in until everything was a speckled, saucy suspension. He tasted and paused, thinking.

"Do you have any chervil?" (I tried to hide a smile as I smugly produced fresh chervil from the fridge—doesn't everyone keep chervil lying around—and, by the way, who IS this clever man?) He chopped a little chervil, stirred it in, and said, "What do you think?"

The vinaigrette was Kim in a teaspoon—smooth, sharp, balanced, complicated, and very delicious. *We were together for six years and are still the best of friends.*

KIM'S TOMATO-SHALLOT VINAIGRETTE

Makes 1 $\frac{1}{3}$ cups (see Note)

$\frac{1}{4}$ cup minced shallot

$\frac{1}{2}$ cup finely minced ripe plum tomatoes

2 garlic cloves, minced

2 tablespoons aged sherry vinegar (see Resources, page 211)

2 tablespoons fresh lemon juice

2 teaspoons kosher salt

1 teaspoon freshly ground black pepper

$\frac{1}{2}$ cup extra virgin olive oil

1 teaspoon minced fresh Italian parsley leaves

1 teaspoon minced fresh chives

1 teaspoon minced fresh tarragon

Optional: Substitute the fresh herbs with 2 teaspoons dried fines herbes

Put the shallot, tomatoes, garlic, vinegar, lemon juice, salt, and pepper in a small bowl, stir to mix, and set aside for 10 minutes. This will give the shallots, tomatoes, and garlic time to give up some of their juices. Then set the bowl on a thick tea towel so it doesn't skid off the counter and slowly pour in the oil while whisking continuously. Add the parsley, chives, and tarragon or dried fines herbes and stir through. This vinaigrette is a bit chunky, so if it's the last thing you make and you're already

dressed for the party, wear a big apron and take care you don't splat the dressing down your front or onto your new blue suede shoes.

Note: If you put the vinaigrette out in a bowl next to the salad, the 1 ⅓ cups will be the right amount, since spooning uses more than tossing. If you plan to toss the salad with vinaigrette, you'll have too much, so only use the amount you need to dress it correctly.

ROAST CAULIFLOWER WITH RAISINS AND THYME
Serves 10

¼ cup plus 1 teaspoon kosher salt

3 heads of cauliflower, at room temperature

⅓ cup extra virgin olive oil

1 teaspoon dried thyme

½ teaspoon freshly ground black pepper

½ cup dark raisins, soaked in hot water for 10 minutes, then drained

1 teaspoon Maldon salt or fleur de sel (see Resources, page 211)

½ teaspoon hot red pepper flakes

¼ cup chopped Italian parsley

Position a rack at the top of the oven and pre-heat to 450°F.

Bring a big saucepan of water with ¼ cup of salt to a boil. Cut the cauliflower into large bite-size pieces, including about an inch of stalk. When the water is at a full rolling boil, add the cauliflower; cover and cook for 5 minutes. Drain and toss very well with the olive oil, 1 teaspoon kosher salt, thyme, and black pepper. Tip onto a sheet pan and roast for 35 to 40 minutes, turning the cauliflower once with a spatula. Cook until some of the edges are golden brown. Remove from the oven and scatter over the raisins, Maldon salt, and hot pepper flakes. Serve hot or at room temperature, strewn with the parsley.

GARLIC BREAD WITH GREEN HERB BUTTER
Makes 2 loaves garlic bread

I love this fragrant green butter and use it on grilled fish, mashed into baked potatoes, or swirled into a bean-filled minestrone.

 garlic cloves, chopped, or to taste

¾ cup packed Italian parsley leaves, chopped

1 ½ cups packed fresh basil leaves, chopped

⅓ cup packed fresh tarragon leaves, chopped

24 tablespoons (3 sticks) unsalted butter, cut into ½-inch cubes, at room temperature

2 teaspoons fresh lemon juice

2 teaspoons kosher salt

2 French baguettes

Put the garlic, parsley, basil, tarragon, butter, lemon juice, and salt in the bowl of a food processor IN THE ORDER LISTED and blend for about 2 minutes, scraping the sides down as needed, until you have a smooth, green-flecked cream.

Position a rack in the upper third of the oven and preheat to 375°F.

Keeping the original shape of the loaves, cut the bread all the way through into 1 1/2-inch diagonal slices. Roll out 2 strips of heavy-duty aluminum foil that are 4 inches longer than the loaves at both ends. Lift the cut bread onto the aluminum foil in sections, re-creating the shape of each loaf. Working from the left and starting with the first actual slice (i.e., not the heel), thickly butter the left side of each slice and press it up against the previous unbuttered slice. When you've finished, wrap the ends of the foil over the bread first, then fold the foil down tightly along the top. Put the wrapped loaves on a sheet pan and bake for 15 minutes, then carefully open up the foil along the top to expose the bread and bake for another 5 to 10 minutes to crisp the crust. Remove the foil and serve the garlic bread hot. If you have extra butter, it freezes beautifully—just roll it into a log, wrap well with plastic, label and date, and use within a month.

Note: Don't be tempted to add thyme or rosemary to the herb butter as they are hard, woody herbs and won't blend smoothly into the mixture. The bread should steam a little while it's baking and there will be melted butter on the bottom, so if you inadvertently rip the foil, start again with another piece or double up.

VENETIAN PEARS
Serves 10

One Easter weekend, I had a house full of people about to play a no-holds-barred Monopoly game, and they wanted me to join them. I won't play Monopoly for fear of being ganged up on, so I used the excuse of working on a recipe to get me out of it. Having trapped myself in the kitchen with no real plan, I looked around to find something to keep me justifiably absent until the game was over. This visually beautiful recipe is the result *and now, sadly, no one ever wants me to play anything. Go and cook, they say.*

Look for Bartlett pears in perfect shape (with a stubby rather than pointy top) and with the stalks left on. If on peeling you find a subcutaneous bruise on one, just put it in the red wine and it will hardly show when it's cooked.

10	firm Bartlett pears, peeled, halved, and cored, keeping the stem intact on one half
6	cups full-bodied red wine
1	tablespoon whole black peppercorns
2 2/3	cups sugar, divided
6	cups full-bodied white wine
1	vanilla bean (see Resources, page 211)
1/2	cup heavy cream, stiffly whipped

Cut a level $1/2$-inch slice off the base of each pear so it will stand up straight. Choose 2 saucepans—one for the red wine and one for the white—both big enough to hold 10 pear halves. Add the red wine, the peppercorns (see Note), half the sugar, and 1 $1/2$ cups water to one pan; add the white wine, vanilla bean, the remaining sugar, and 1 $1/2$ cups of water to the other pan. Bring each pan to a slow boil and reduce the liquid for 5 minutes. Add the pears, making sure you have FIVE of the ones with stems in the red wine and FIVE with stems in the white. Cover and simmer for 30 to 40 minutes, depending on the ripeness of the pears. When a toothpick enters without too much resistance, remove from the heat and set aside to cool. Refrigate overnight.

When you come to arrange the pears on a platter, take 1 red pear half WITH a stalk and 1 white half WITHOUT, and then vice versa; sandwich them together carefully with a tablespoon of the whipped cream.

Note: Don't worry about the peppercorns—just let them rattle around in the pan and pick off any stuck to the pears after cooking. I leave them soaking in the syrup since they taste rather wonderful plumped up as they are . . . full of wine and sugar.

FREE-FORM PLUM, ROSEMARY, AND ORANGE CROSTATA
Serves 10 to 12

A word to the wise—the quality of the plums is key in this recipe. They must be firm—if they aren't, they'll exude too much juice and you'll be pouring plum soup into a flat pastry shell, and you won't be happy with me or this recipe. I use an Analon wok to sauté the plums (see Resources, page 211). It's just the right size, nonstick, and nice and heavy. This is such a fabulous recipe, but it does require some understanding of the procedures, so do read the four notes at the end of this recipe before you start.

THE PASTRY

2 1/2 cups Heckers or King Arthur all-purpose flour, plus extra for rolling the dough

1 teaspoon kosher salt

4 tablespoons sugar, divided

16 tablespoons (2 sticks) unsalted butter, cut into 1/2-inch cubes and chilled

1/2 cup iced water (filled to the rim)

1 egg white, whisked lightly with a fork

Put the flour, salt, and 3 tablespoons of the sugar into the bowl of a food processor, then scatter on the cubes of chilled butter. Pulse 10 times, then pour in the water while pulsing another 10 to 12 times. The mixture should be crumbly (not in any way formed into a ball) and have pea-size chunks of butter visible. Tip into a baggie and set aside to rest for 5 minutes. This resting time will allow the water to dampen the flour so the dough will hold together well. Gather up the plastic and gently but firmly press the crumb into an evenly thick 7-inch disk. Refrigerate for at least 2 hours, or overnight. (The dough can also be well wrapped with plastic wrap and frozen for up to 2 months. Just be sure to label it well so you don't grab this sweet pastry and use it for a savory recipe.)

When you take the pastry out of the fridge, let it soften for 20 minutes so it won't crack when you roll it out. Roll the pastry out onto a lightly floured surface to a 14-inch diameter circle. Slide a cookie sheet under the pastry. Lightly

fold the edge over by 3/4 inch and then over again. Crimp the pastry casually to form a slightly raised rim.

Brush the rim of the tart with the egg white and sprinkle with the remaining tablespoon of sugar. Prick the base with a fork, making sure the tines completely penetrate, and put the pastry on the cookie sheet in the refrigerator for 30 minutes.

Position a rack in the middle of the oven and preheat to 425°F.

Take the pastry out of the fridge and bake for 20 to 25 minutes, or until it's fully cooked and a crisp golden brown (see Notes 1 and 2). Remove from the oven and set aside, then turn the oven temperature down to 350°F.

THE PLUM FILLING

- 1/2 cup sugar, plus 1 tablespoon for sprinkling on top
- 2 tablespoons unsalted butter
- 1 1/2 teaspoons minced rosemary leaves
- 3 strips orange zest, julienned
- 2 1/2 pounds firm red or black plums, pitted and quartered (see Note 3)

Put a large nonstick wok or sauté pan over medium heat on your biggest burner for 2 minutes. Add the sugar, butter, rosemary, and orange zest. Turn the heat to high and cook for 1 1/2 minutes, or until the sugar starts to caramelize, then add the plums. The sugar in the pan might seize up and form nuggets, but keep the heat high, flipping the fruit up and over on itself every now and then for about 7 minutes, and it will all come together. The aim is for translucent, just-cooked slices in a little syrup (see Note 4). Tip the contents of the saucepan into the pastry shell, allowing the plums to form their own random pattern, sprinkle with 1 tablespoon sugar, and bake for 35 minutes. Serve either warm or at room temperature with vanilla ice cream or slightly sweetened whipped cream.

Note 1: Check the base after the first 10 minutes as this shell is baked without any paper and beans to keep it flat. If it's ballooning up, poke the pastry with the point of a small knife to release the air and press it gently back down with a metal spatula.

Note 2: You must have the tart shell ready by the time the fruit is done—if the plums have to wait to go in the oven, too much juice will seep out of them.

Note 3: To pit the plums, cut around the plum following the natural line running from the stem. Hold the plum with both hands and twist each side in the opposite direction. The pit will still be on one of the sides—just cut around it with a small knife to remove it.

Note 4: If you have a lot of syrup, lift out the plums with a slotted spoon and put them in the pastry shell, boil the juices down to 1/3 cup, and pour evenly over the plums making sure you don't overflow the pastry rim.

WHATEVER DANA WANTS STORY When you cook for a living and would like all your potential clients out there to think you are wise and well-informed, you develop a delicate symbiosis with the press. You want them to promote you and your wares and they want an interesting story, recipe, or tip. In order not to waste anyone's time, if a journalist calls with a special request, you have to come up with something, or you'll lose the opportunity—and it better be good, and it better be fast. So, *Food & Wine* magazine called on a Thursday morning wanting to feature a tart that I had taken to the editor Dana Cowin's house for dinner several months earlier. Even though it was a very glamorous dinner for the filmmaker Ismail Merchant, when I had called to accept I said I would love to bring a dessert since on the whole, I can't bear to turn up anywhere without bringing something that I've cooked myself. Dana said OK. It was a wonderful party, and, thank God, everyone loved my tart.

Back to the Thursday morning tart duplication request . . . Well, the fact is that, as I zoom past fifty (age), the memory, which was a pretty loosely woven net in the first place, currently has about three threads intact, which catch only the most life-threatening information. I am longing for grandchildren to come along, as they will remember everything. No doubt the missing grandchildren would have known what kind of tart I had taken, but I certainly didn't. I felt anxious that if I couldn't supply exactly the same thing, the September back page of a national magazine would be full of someone else's tart. Unless . . . if I could only invent something . . . something so spectacular . . . my mind was racing . . . they would like the new idea EVEN BETTER.

"ActuallyI'mnotahundredpercentsurewhatDana'startwaslike."—*I brushed the old tart aside*—"But . . . " still thinking, " . . . we were just working on the most fabulous thing for fall. Yes! . . . It's with those divine, big red plums . . . kind of . . ." (hmm . . . kind of what?) "CARAMELIZED, yes caramelized with rosemary, . . . " (I sensed questioning going on, down the phone line) ". . . cut very, very small, of course. It's quite modern, very Jean-Georges, we found it needed something . . . to balance it . . . to balance the herbal thing, so we tried . . . er, we tried . . . ORANGE PEEL(!), julienned, of course, and it was absolutely delicious." Great interest on the phone now, so I plowed on. "You can't imagine how fantastic it is."

"Well, this sounds amazing. So when can I get the recipe?" she asked. "Oh, the recipe . . . um—how about tomorrow?" The happy editor: *"That'll be just wonderful."*

Now, what's odd is that even though the idea had been conjured up out of thin air, the concept was so fully realized in my mind that the tart—now a crostata because it's flat—worked perfectly the first time I made it, which was a huge relief.

SPEAKING ENGLISH

Heavy white lace or linen cloth

Full-blown mixed garden roses with trailing ivy

Mason's Ironstone or Leedsware platters

Silver candelabra

Pimm's Cup (see page 94)

Cutglass bowls

Salmon Fillets Stuffed with Glazed Balsamic Onions

Ham with Supernal Mustard and Parsley Sauce

Tomato Towers and Crab with Aïoli

Green Lettuces with Deep Woods Dressing

New Potatoes and Mint

Tender Green Beans

Summer Pudding

Peaches with Sauternes Sabayon

BUFFETS IN ENGLAND

Buffets are not that common in England; we prefer to all sit around a table for Sunday lunch and have a good chat. But when you do come across a buffet in an English home, it will probably be a beautiful thing. I tend to drag out all the old silver and exquisitely embroidered tablecloths from my first mother-in-law (she had the best stuff) and polish up any silver of my own. I like a gleaming table. The food in this menu is pretty too, with the pink salmon and ham, the pale golden mustard sauce, and citrine lettuces. If you have ransacked the garden or flower shops for full-blown pink and pale yellow roses to deck the table with (NOT the military, Valentine's Day kind) then, when dessert comes out, the crimson summer pudding and the creamy peaches and sabayon will be almost too much to bear—they'll look so gorgeous. What I love here is the combination of an elegant and even old-fashioned, English country house kind of a table, with simple classic food.

SALMON FILLETS STUFFED WITH GLAZED BALSAMIC ONIONS

Serves 12 with leftovers

This recipe calls for two whole salmon fillets sandwiched with melted sweet and sour onions. It's one of the best recipes I make, and I know when you're eating it you'll feel the same way. Have the fishmonger skin and debone a whole fish for you. I love the caterpillar look that the string tied every two inches leaves, and I very much like the fact that the salmon, when layered with the onions, is so thick that the edges get caramelized, while the middle stays delicate and juicy.

When I get down to making the onions, I set a timer, and—racing against the clock—aim to get them all sliced in ten minutes or so. *Something has to keep my mind focused, otherwise I get bored, I cry, I wander off and answer the phone with oniony hands.* (Grace Jones's CD *Island Life*, or a little Scarlatti helps the pace.)

THE GLAZED BALSAMIC ONIONS

1/3 cup extra virgin olive oil

10 thinly sliced firm red onions

1 tablespoon minced garlic

1/2 cup packed dark brown sugar

1/2 cup balsamic vinegar

1 1/2 tablespoons loosely packed fresh thyme leaves (or 2 teaspoons dried)

Position a rack at the top of the oven and preheat to 375°F.

Put the largest sauté pan you have over high heat and add the olive oil and onions. (If your pan isn't big enough, you might have to cook half the onions and then repeat the process in the same pan, or use 2 pans.) Cook the onions, stirring occasionally, for 10 minutes, or until they are translucent, then add the garlic, brown sugar, vinegar, and thyme. Continue cooking, stirring every now and then, for 10 minutes. Transfer the glazed onions to an ungreased, unlined sheet pan and put in the oven for 50 minutes, stirring once. When the onions come out of the oven, scrape up the caramelized edges so they don't set like a rock.

You can get to this point up to 2 days ahead and store these onions in the fridge—just bring them to room temperature before stuffing the salmon—or you'll affect the cooking time.

THE SALMON

8 tablespoons (1 stick) unsalted butter, softened

One 10-pound salmon, skinned, filleted, and pin-boned (see Note)

2 tablespoons kosher salt

2 teaspoons freshly ground black pepper

Watercress, for decoration

Position a rack in the middle of the oven and preheat to 350°F.

Rub the butter into all sides of the 2 salmon fillets and sprinkle with the salt and pepper. Lay the bottom fillet down on an ungreased, unlined sheet pan, then arrange the cooled balsamic onions evenly on top. Cover with the other fillet and tie the whole salmon with string every 2 inches.

Bake for 45 minutes. The edges of the fish and the visible onions will be beautifully caramelized. Let the fish rest for 10 minutes,

then, using 2 large spatulas or a cookie sheet, transfer it carefully to the platter you want to serve it on and remove the string. You have to move fast if you're using spatulas or get another person to help support the middle of the fish. Serve warm or at room temperature, decorated with a flourish of watercress.

This recipe can be converted to individual portions by cutting the salmon into 6-ounce pieces, rubbing with butter, salt, and pepper,

then arranging some onions on each portion. Bake for 10 to 12 minutes, depending on the thickness of the fish.

Note: To pinbone the salmon effortlessly, use needle-nose pliers. Run your finger down the middle of each fillet and you'll feel the small pin bones in a line, just sticking out of the flesh. Pull the bones out at a low angle, in the direction they're embedded, almost level with the surface of the fish so the flesh doesn't tear.

HAM WITH MUSTARD AND PARSLEY SAUCE
Serves 12, with leftovers

There's something wonderfully medieval about cross-hatching the ham with a sharp knife and studding it with a veil of cloves. Then you get to slather the ham with a gorgeous mess of orange marmalade, fresh ginger, sharp Dijon mustard, and damp, dark brown sugar, which caramelize in the oven, making particularly addictive little crusty bits. Speaking personally, I've decided it's the cook's prerogative to pull off those pieces and eat them before anyone else gets a look in.

THE HAM

7 pounds smoked ham (about half a whole ham) on the bone, major fat trimmed (see Resources, page 211)

About 30 whole cloves (try to pick ones with the round seed still on top)

Supernal Mustard and Parsley Sauce (recipe follows)

Position a rack in the lower third of the oven and preheat to 375°F.

If you have a Silpat pan liner (see Resources, page 211), this is the perfect time to use it. Lay it in a sheet pan and set aside. Or just grease the pan well. Using a sharp knife, crosshatch the ham in 1 1/2-inch diamonds and stud each cross with a clove.

THE MARMALADE MESS MARINADE

1/2 cup Orange Marmalade (see recipe, page 19, or use any commercial brand)

1/4 cup fresh ginger, peeled and grated

2 teaspoons crushed garlic

4 teaspoons Dijon mustard

1/2 cup packed dark brown sugar

1/2 teaspoon freshly ground black pepper

Mix all the marinade ingredients together in a small bowl. Place the ham facedown on the Silpat and spread the marinade over the surface. Put the ham in the oven and bake for 8 minutes per pound. After 30 minutes, baste with any marinade that's on the base of the pan. Remove the ham from the oven, and if you're serving it hot, transfer it to a hot serving dish and allow it to rest in a warm place, uncovered, for 15 to 20 minutes. *Unless it's put in an icy gale it will still be warm in the middle and the juices will have time to settle back into the meat.*

When you come to serve the ham, you can either carve it in the kitchen and pile the slices on a beautiful platter or present the ham on a spiked wooden carving board and carve it in public as needed. If you're serving it at room temperature, set it aside for up to 6 hours, unrefrigerated, then carve the way you would the hot ham. Serve with a bowl of Supernal Mustard and Parsley Sauce.

If there aren't many people around to eat the leftover ham . . . and after a few days you can't bear to look at it one moment longer, you can take the meat off the bone and freeze it and the bone, separately. *(Remember Dorothy Parker's definition of eternity . . . "Two people and a ham.")*

The meat can be used in a frittata, in risotto with peas and mint; it can be added to a macaroni and cheese, or a chopped cupful could be folded into Guadalajara Hash (see recipe, page 43) 10 minutes before it's finished cooking. The possibilities are probably endless. Simmer the bone in a split pea and marjoram OR white bean and rosemary soup. It can be used to lend flavor at least twice. Just rinse the bone, wrap, and refreeze it.

SUPERNAL MUSTARD AND PARSLEY SAUCE

Makes 1 1/2 cups

I suppose this sauce isn't rocket science, but I think it's special because the balance is very good and all the ingredients work together.

Pungent mustard is the ringleader—then as you bite on a little piece of shallot or a nugget of salt, everything comes into play. This is one of the times to be PARTICULARLY fussy about ingredients. Look for or order fleur de sel (see Resources, page 211), a fancy sea salt from France; its large crystals don't dissolve in the sauce and it's delicious to bite on. If the shallot isn't rock-solid, you won't be able to cut perfect little dice; the parsley has to be alert and full of juice, and the mustard can't just be the residue of three nearly empty jars that have been skulking in the fridge for six months. Grey Poupon or the Dijon mustard from Williams-Sonoma are the best widely available mustards. Be sure to cut the shallots into tiny dice—they mustn't be minced for this sauce, or would become overpowering.

1/4   cup Dijon mustard

1/3   cup finely diced shallots

1   teaspoon minced garlic

1/2   teaspoon freshly coarsely ground black pepper

1/2   cup golden olive oil at room temperature

1/2   cup packed minced Italian parsley, with some smaller crunchy stems

2   teaspoons fleur de sel (see Resources, page 211), or kosher salt

In a small bowl, mix together the mustard, shallots, and garlic. Grind in the pepper in the roughest pieces possible without actual peppercorns dropping out of your grinder. Very slowly whisk in the olive oil in a thin stream, as you would for a mayonnaise, then stir in the parsley. Add the salt last; if you do that, it will become suspended in the oil and—particularly if you use the fleur de sel—stay discernable in the sauce.

Note: To convert any leftovers to a vinaigrette, add some lemon juice and whisk in more olive oil until you have the right consistency.

TOMATO TOWERS AND CRAB WITH AÏOLI
Makes 16 towers

This pretty little dish is easier to make than it looks and can be prepared entirely the day before and put together an hour before the party. The tomato part is in fact just gazpacho delicately set with gelatin and (if it's a relaxed party) is an ideal dish to ask friends to help with assembly. You can tell them all about how the tomato towers are made, then there will be at least two or three people among the guests who know what they're looking at, since we're dangerously close to the "mystery food" mentioned on page 99. The jumbo lump crabmeat is rich but tempered perfectly by the aïoli and the aged sherry vinegar in the tomato juice. I use little metal dariole molds from Williams-Sonoma (but you could use anything with about a one-third-cup volume), then I turn the tomato tower out and stick a bold herb on top.

2 packets plus 1 teaspoon Knox powdered gelatin

3 ½ cups Sacramento brand tomato juice

½ cup English cucumber, unpeeled, in ⅛-inch dice

½ cup seeded Holland red pepper, in ⅛-inch dice

1 tablespoon seeded, minced jalapeño pepper (or to taste)

¼ cup scallions, white part only, cut lengthways in quarters, then in ⅛-inch slices

1 minced clove garlic

1 tablespoon minced fresh basil leaves

2 tablespoons aged sherry vinegar

2 teaspoons kosher salt

½ teaspoon freshly ground black pepper

Crab with Aïoli (see recipe, page 134)

1 bunch perfect basil, for decoration

Marcona almonds for scattering (see Resources, page 211)

Pour ⅓ cup of water in a small saucepan and sprinkle on the powdered gelatin in an even layer. Set aside to soften for at least 10 minutes.

Put the tomato juice in a medium bowl; add the cucumber, red pepper, jalapeño, scallions, garlic, basil, vinegar, salt, and pepper; stir well and set aside. Back to the softening gelatin: Set the pan over a low heat. (Don't let the gelatin boil, or it won't set properly.) When the gelatin mixture is totally liquid, about 1 minute, pour it into the tomato juice and vegetables, stirring quickly to incorporate.

Spray 16 individual molds with vegetable oil and fill with the tomato mixture. Place the filled molds on a tray, cover loosely with plastic wrap, and refrigerate overnight. One or two hours before your guests arrive, rub the serving platter you're using lightly with vegetable oil—then if a tomato tower lands in the wrong spot you can slide it over. Remove the molds from the fridge and dip them in a pan of very hot tap water for 2 or 3 seconds. Turn them over and free the gelatin by tapping the mold sharply on the serving platter. Keep the towers refrigerated until they go out on the buffet. Up to half an hour before serving, surround the towers with jumbo lump Crab with Aïoli, (see recipe, page 134) and sprinkle with almonds. Stick a sprig or a couple of leaves of basil on top. Provide a thin, square, metal spatula for a serving utensil. It will make the tomato towers easier to access, and the platter won't look like a train wreck, as it might very well do with a spoon and fork.

AÏOLI FOR JULIA STORY In my case, the phrase "charity is its own reward" developed into "charity has its own reward." I had shelled out some mighty (tax-deductible) dollars benefiting the New York City Ballet and had gone to a lunch at Lincoln Center where I was at the editor of *Food & Wine* magazine, Dana Cowin's, table. The table was dotted with foody people and Dorothy Hamilton, who started New York City's French Culinary Institute, was seated three to my right. This is my official apology to the two people between us, as Dorothy and I kept up a running conversation throughout the whole lunch and could have justifiably been branded as quite socially inept.

We subsequently became dear friends, even though I am secretly a bit intimidated by the fact that she knows absolutely everyone in the food world—*very well*. I've spent many weekends with Dorothy and her family in their country house; then when I bought my own house in Connecticut, I became reclusive and hard to budge, but one day we were talking on the phone and she said, "Why don't you come for lunch on Sunday? . . . Julia will be there." I agreed to go immediately, *as what could be more thrilling than to eat with Julia Child?* I thought about all the dishes I had made from her seminal book *Mastering the Art of French Cooking.* I still have a first edition, bought in 1962, and I remembered how I had loved learning culinary skills and lore from her. I could hardly wait to meet her.

Sunday was a mild and sunny day, and as I drove, I wondered what I would have cooked for Julia if she'd been coming to my house. I considered and rejected all the things I make best; no one thing seemed good enough for the muse of my favorite art.

When I got to Dorothy's house, she and her husband were just sitting around reading the newspapers—obviously whatever we were eating for lunch was basking in its marinade and everything else was already made. No sign of Julia, so I took the *Times* crossword puzzle and went to lie in the hammock. A little while later, Dorothy wandered over and said casually, "So, what shall we have for lunch . . . ? I have fresh tuna . . ." I leapt out of the hammock, *"Whaddayamean—it's not all ready?"* My anxious face made her laugh. "Don't worry, Julia's easy and I've done a couple of things." The *couple of things* were cooking little fingerling potatoes and haricots verts from the garden and picking some antique variety of tomatoes she'd grown from seed that were streaked with fuchsia and purple.

We walked back to the house and found Julia standing in the hall with Dorothy's husband. I went to be introduced. I was captivated and felt as though I could have stared into her blue eyes forever. I couldn't let go of her large, firm, liver-spotted hand and put my other hand on it as well, to silently let her know what a HUGE BIG DEAL it was for me to meet her, while I blathered on about the weather.

The lunch table—set away from the house in tree-dappled sunshine on the edge of a lake—was already laid, so all we had to do was make the food. We looked at our ingredients; clearly a Niçoise salad was the way to go. I offered to make an aïoli, as I wanted to actually create something rather than just arrange vegetables, however impeccable. The tuna (after half an hour in a lemony marinade) was grilled outside over coals and grapevine cuttings; the potatoes, haricots verts, and gaudy wedges of tomato were scattered with oil-cured black olives. The aïoli—shimmering with garlic—was passed around the table in a red bowl. It was the best I'd ever made, possibly the result of the heathen incantations I'd muttered with every pound of the pestle, as I tried to invoke perfection so *she* would like it. (More likely due to the squeaky-fresh purple garlic, Dijon mustard from France, and golden olive oil in an elegant foil-wrapped bottle.) We set upon the food, commenting endlessly upon its excellence and our great good fortune. When everything else was gone, the red bowl was duly wiped clean, first with French bread and then with index fingers.

"My goodness . . . that was awfully nice aïoli," said Julia.

Dorothy's coffee granita scented with sambuca was the dessert, possibly the most delicious thing I've ever eaten, especially as it was partnered with a good dollop of whipped cream.

I drove home in an ecstatic state and just imagine: if I hadn't been charitable, there would have been no friendship, no Julia, no story, no nothing.

CRAB WITH AÏOLI
Serves 10

This is not exactly a classic aïoli, as it has no bread in it, and I've added mustard, but it's awfully good and worth buying a mortar and pestle to make it with if you haven't already got one. Made that way, you end up with a beautiful oily suspension that's almost translucent like quartz, and lands with a sexy quiver when dropped off a spoon.

Since there are only a few ingredients in an aïoli, and two of them are salt and pepper, the others better be first-rate.

There is no point making this without a very good quality olive oil, firm garlic, sharp Dijon mustard, and good quality, strongly acidic vinegar. I lke sherry vinegar that's been aged for thirty or so years (see Resources, page 211) so that two teaspoons will be sufficient. If the vinegar isn't powerful, you'll have to use too much and the aïoli will be thin. It's also important for the olive oil, egg yolks, mustard, and vinegar to be at room temperature.

1 cup high-quality olive oil

2 garlic cloves

1/2 teaspoon kosher salt

2 extra-large egg yolks

1 teaspoon Dijon mustard, preferably Grey Poupon or Maille

1/4 teaspoon freshly ground black pepper

2 teaspoons aged sherry vinegar

1 pound jumbo lump crabmeat

USING A MORTAR AND PESTLE

Measure the oil into a little pitcher that pours well without dribbling. Put the garlic and salt in the bowl of the mortar and, using the pestle, pound them to a smooth puree. Add the egg yolks and again using the pestle, work them with the garlic and the salt for a full minute, until they're thick and sticky. Add the mustard, and pepper and blend in well. Add half of the olive oil, drop by drop, until the sauce has thickened considerably, then add 1 teaspoon of the vinegar, which will loosen it.

Mix the vinegar in well, then start pouring the rest of the olive oil in a very thin stream, mixing with the pestle constantly. Finally, add the remaining teaspoon of vinegar and mix it in well. If you're using red wine vinegar instead of aged sherry vinegar, you might feel the acidic balance is not strong enough—in that case, add another 1/2 teaspoon of vinegar, but no more or the sauce will be too thin.

USING A BOWL AND BALLOON WHISK

On a cutting board, roughly chop the garlic and sprinkle on the salt. Turn the knife nearly flat and crush the garlic away from you bit by bit with the blade, using your other hand to lend weight and to push down and away. Scrape the garlic all together and crush it away from you a few more times, to a fine puree.

Put the garlic puree in a bowl and proceed as above, whisking for a full minute to turn the eggs yolks thick and sticky, then adding the mustard, pepper, oil, and vinegar, in that order. The finished sauce will look more opaque than the one made with a pestle and taste a little creamier because of the incorporation of air.

TO FINISH

Tip the crab out of its container into a shallow bowl and put another medium bowl next to the first. Pick through the crab very carefully, feeling for any shells or cartilage with your fingertips but trying not to crush the large lumps of crab. Put the cleaned crab in the second bowl as it passes muster. Gently fold the aïoli through the crab, then spoon it around the tomato towers on their platter.

Scatter the Marcona almonds (leave them whole or chop them up a bit, you choose), around the towers over the Crab with Aïoli.

GREEN LETTUCES WITH DEEP WOODS DRESSING
Makes 1 cup

When I lived in North Salem, I had dinner one night with an antique dealer friend who lived in an enormous barn in the woods—surrounded by expensive American furniture. All the tables, chairs, and sideboards were plain but fine, with a fragrance and sheen resulting from hours of diligence with homemade beeswax polish—as I was informed.

I sat down for dinner somewhat expecting a virtuous Amish stew, but a salad of exquisitely tender Boston lettuce with a mysteriously dark, herb-flecked dressing began the meal. Conversation was rowdy as I put the first bite in my mouth and so "EXCUSE ME!" I was forced to bellow. "What is on this lettuce, EXACTLY?"

I wanted to possess the knowledge immediately. I wanted to have the ability to reproduce it inscribed neatly in my recipe book, for all eternity. It was herbal, sharp, sweet, and deep, a combination that—what with all the noise and my state of excitement—I couldn't immediately decipher. In fact, the recipe proved to contain no exotica, it was just the unexpected combinations that had surprised and delighted me, as I hope it will you, too.

Boston lettuce is quite delicate, so when it's going on a buffet, I mix it with pale but sturdy hearts of frisée to give it some support.

3 tablespoons balsamic vinegar

1 tablespoon Dijon mustard

1 tablespoon honey

2 garlic cloves, crushed

3/4 teaspoon kosher salt

1/2 teaspoon freshly ground black pepper

3/4 cup basil olive oil (see Note)

1 to 2 heads frisée, trimmed of any dark outer leaves

2 to 3 heads Boston lettuce, trimmed of any dark or damaged outer leaves

1/4 cup loosely packed fresh basil (the leaves torn into rough pieces)

In a small bowl, whisk together the vinegar, mustard, honey, garlic, salt, and pepper, then slowly whisk in the basil oil and set aside. In a large bowl mix together the frisée, Boston lettuce, and basil. Pack loosely in Ziploc bags and refrigerate until serving time.

Just before you put out the salad, toss with the dressing; it tastes much better lightly tossed rather than spooned heavily on by guests at the buffet.

Note: Basil oil can either be bought (see Resources, page 211) or made very easily at home. Blend 1 cup chilled olive oil, 1/2 cup packed clean, dry basil leaves, and 1/2 teaspoon kosher salt for one minute. Strain and use as needed. This recipe is directly from the maestro—Mario Batali.

POTATOES AT TWILIGHT STORY The French like chives with their potatoes, the Italians and Greeks favor rosemary, Americans love parsley and scallions, but the English go for mint. I can't think of another mouthful of food, which would more immediately place me at an English table than tiny, little potatoes in a pool of butter, flecked with fresh mint, and dusted with flakes of Maldon salt.

I had dear friends, Bob and Jill, who bought a beautiful Georgian house outside the town of Oxford in England. I went to stay with them often, and meals were always interesting. Whether it was coming down to breakfast to find their oldest son trying to make opium from poppy pods on the Aga—"At least he's UP," remarked Jill—or at dinner, being careful of what you said because any mention of Chaucer would elicit a two-minute recitation by Bob from the Canterbury Tales, in the original "olde" English. One could only listen in amazement. Obviously, he was wildly eccentric—not surprising for the son of an inventor—and had terribly grand ideas. Every time I visited their house, he and I would wander the HUGE garden and he'd sweep his arm out, indicating, for instance, where fifteen hundred dwarf boxwood

shrubs were going to be planted next week to extend the parterre. Or he'd point to a nearby field and describe "the new stable wing." I would nod with narrow eyes and a thoughtful frown. I breathed many "I seeeee-s" and was very impressed, anticipating the magnificence.

But in truth, the most wonderful thing was their walled acre of vegetable garden with espaliered fruit trees standing at attention around the perimeter. The soft-fruited trees were planted against ancient red brick walls that held the heat of the sun and the apple trees were trained over arched hoops, creating walkways from the carrots to the kale. The garden itself contained manicured rows of endless variety; not just beans, for instance, but wax beans, haricots verts, scarlet runners, yellow beans, broad beans; not just lettuce, but at least ten varieties, of which the taciturn, old head gardener and his four strapping assistants had staggered the planting, so they wouldn't all be ready at the same time, creating a terrible glut.

We were dispatched one evening to dig potatoes for dinner. A heavy dew drenched our shoes, some cows were stamping and flicking their tails across the valley, and a low sickle moon was rising in an opalescent sky.

Bob—an old trug basket over his arm and a small garden spade (the fork had gone missing) in his hand—swung open the wrought-iron gate to the vegetable garden. A pair of pheasants whirred up from under our feet. I said "AAAAAGH!" but Bob marched obliviously on to the potatoes. We stood gazing at rows of green leaves, and he started a monologue about exactly what we were eating for dinner and which particular potato would be the happiest choice. He dismissed the Epicures and the Pink Fir Apples and reared his spade over the Rattes. The soil was as well-behaved as everything else, and the metal sank in easily; Bob started lifting little tubers by the dozen. I picked them out of the soil and dropped handfuls of damp potatoes into Bob's dilapidated trug basket, which he said he'd made in wood-working class at school, some forty years ago. As we left, he bent and with a penknife cut a sheaf of mint to go with the potatoes; its perfume filled the night air and mingled with the smell of the soil and Bob's Harris Tweed jacket.

Possibly the trug basket had seen better days, but I don't think I had.

NEW POTATOES AND MINT
Serves 10 (see photograph, page 128)

4 pounds small, evenly sized white potatoes, washed but not peeled

2 tablespoons kosher salt

8 tablespoons (1 stick) unsalted butter, at room temperature

1/4 cup loosely packed fresh mint leaves

2 teaspoons Maldon salt or fleur de sel (see Resources, page 211)

1/2 teaspoon freshly ground black pepper

Put the potatoes and kosher salt in a large saucepan and just cover them with cold water. Bring to a simmer over medium heat. Cook, covered, for 15 to 20 minutes, then start testing for doneness by inserting a small, sharp knife into a potato. When they're ready (it's hard to give an accurate time, as there's such a wide variable), the potatoes should be firmly cooked, not soft. Drain and set aside for 5 to 10 minutes. The potatoes will steam away any surface water and cool slightly so when you toss them with the butter, the butter will adhere to their surface more readily. Toss the potatoes with the butter and mint. Serve scattered with the Maldon salt and pepper.

TENDER GREEN BEANS
Serves 10

You might think haricots verts, those little French beans, are the tenderest beans to buy and (unless you can find freshly picked green beans at a farm stand) you're probably right.

Just don't vastly undercook them, as so often is the case with well-intentioned people who aim to preserve the vitamins. What happens is that the beans end up with nasty, spiky little tails—like something they might expect you to eat on *Fear Factor*.

- 3 1/2   pounds haricots verts or young green beans, trimmed
- 2   tablespoons kosher salt
- 2   tablespoons extra virgin olive oil OR 2 tablespoons (1/4 stick) unsalted butter
- 1   teaspoon Maldon salt or fleur de sel (see Resources, page 211)
- 1/2   teaspoon freshly ground black pepper

Line a sheet pan with paper towels and set aside. Bring a large saucepan of water to a boil. Add the green beans and the kosher salt to the saucepan. Cook until al dente, 3 to 6 minutes. Strain and run under cold water to stop the cooking, then spread the beans on the paper towels to air dry. EITHER dress with the olive oil, Maldon salt, and pepper and serve at room temperature OR toss with the butter in a large saucepan over medium heat until the beans are hot, then add the Maldon salt and the pepper.

SUMMER PUDDING
Serves 10

In England, summer pudding almost always includes tart black currants and super-tart red currants. They are pretty hard to find here in America, but I've made a version without them and it's still mouth-wateringly addictive. We (the English) wouldn't serve this with whipped cream, but rather with heavy cream (or for the boss, Devonshire clotted cream, see Resources, page 211) poured from a pitcher—which usually has to be refilled at least once—as English people DO like their cream.

The transmutation of bread into a soggy vertical wall strong enough (after turning out) to contain masses of cooked berries and enough of their juice to thoroughly imbue the bread is very interesting.

It's difficult to arrive at alchemy of this ilk by guesswork, so I've determined four pointers for success:

1 Using good peasant bread without any big holes, sliced evenly and thinly
2 Cooking the blueberries long enough so they produce sufficient juice
3 Using an approximately 4-pound weight to press the pudding
4 Leaving the pudding long enough under the weight (at the very least for 24 hours and ideally, 2 days)

None of this is difficult—in fact, once you get going it's tremendously easy.

1   loaf fine-grain peasant bread, sliced
    1/3 inch thick, crusts trimmed

5   cups blueberries, divided

1   cup sugar

4   cups strawberries, trimmed and
    sliced 1/3 inch thick

5   cups raspberries, divided

3/4   teaspoon rose water (optional)

1   bunch beautiful mint, for decoration
    Heavy cream

The ideal container is a white ceramic 2-quart soufflé dish. Line the dish with two strips of plastic wrap (one down and one across) with about 5 inches overhang at each end.

Cut the bread to fit closely in the base of the dish. Start cutting rectangles of bread, which (when resting on the bread already in the dish) will come just to the rim. Trim the rectangle a tiny bit narrower at the lower end to allow for the slope of the dish. You're building

a bread wall that should fit perfectly when it's finished, without any gaps or buckling—very couture. When it's done, set it aside.

Wash the blueberries, put 4 cups of them in a medium saucepan and pour on the sugar. Cover the pan and set over medium heat. It will take about 5 minutes for the blueberries to start releasing their juices; then lower the heat and simmer for about another 3 minutes. The pan should be full of juice with blueberries floating in it. Throw in the strawberries and simmer for another 2 minutes, then remove from the heat and fold in 4 cups of the raspberries. Add the rose water and pour the mixture straight into the bread-lined dish. With any luck it will fit perfectly.

Cut bread to cover the surface. Flip the ends of plastic wrap over the top, and press down a few times to start the juices soaking into the bread. Find a flat plate or anything that fits inside the dish and can sink down unobstructed. Put the dish in a nonreactive cake pan or something with a rim, as juices could overflow. Set a 4-pound weight on top and put in the fridge. Leave for at least 24 hours and ideally two days. Check on the weight a couple of times, as it might shift and press unevenly.

TO UN-MOLD

Remove the weight and the plate. Clean the dish, cut off the excess plastic wrap with scissors, and turn the pudding over onto a platter. Holding the dish and platter together, shake them down firmly twice, then remove the dish slowly. The plastic-wrap liner makes this a cinch. Leave the plastic wrap on until serving time; it will keep the pudding juicy.

Mix the additional blueberries and raspberries and pile them on the pudding, setting a little bunch of mint prettily behind them. Serve with heavy cream.

PEACHES WITH SAUTERNES SABAYON
Serves 10

If you can find those exquisite white peaches with ruby blushed skin and a perfume that makes your mouth water, then this dish will succeed beyond comprehension. Not many things are elegant and fun, but treating this fancy sabayon as a chic dip for assorted summer fruits on skewers, such as nectarines, apricots, strawberries, and muscat grapes becomes just that.

I have also made the sabayon by substituting $1/2$ cup Calvados for the Sauternes and served it in the autumn with a compote of blackberries and Braeburn apples poached with a vanilla bean. And that's spectacular.

- $1/2$ cup sugar
- 6 extra-large egg yolks
- 1 cup Sauternes, such as Muscat de Baumes de Venise
- 1 cup heavy cream
- 8 white-fleshed peaches or assorted summer fruits

THE SABAYON
Using a handheld electric mixer, whisk together the sugar, yolks, and Sauternes in a heavy stainless steel bowl, then set the bowl over a saucepan containing 3 inches of simmering water. Beat over the water until the mixture is thick and voluminous, about 5 minutes, then cool over a bowl of ice, stirring occasionally. Whip the heavy cream to soft peaks and fold into the Sauternes mixture. Put in a beautiful bowl, cover, and refrigerate overnight. Serve with the peaches.

THE PEACHES
Bring a medium-size saucepan of water to a boil, then remove from the heat. With a sharp knife, cut a small, shallow cross on the base of each peach and drop 1 peach into the hot water. Wait about 15 to 30 seconds and remove with a slotted spoon. See if the skin has loosened enough to peel off easily. If not, give the peach another 30 seconds in the water, then try again. Repeat the process with all the peaches. You might have to reboil the water after the first few.

When they're all peeled, cut with a small, sharp knife around each peach, starting at the stalk end and following the natural depression. Holding the peach with both hands, twist the halves in opposite directions to separate. Remove the pit and cut each half into thick slices. Pile the peach slices into a cutglass dish and serve with the sabayon. If the peaches refuse to separate, just cut the peeled peach off the pit in thick uneven slices—they'll be just as wonderful.

SPEAKING AMERICAN

Large glass vases of red flowers (lilies, gerberas, tulips, even massed scarlet carnations)

A blue-and-white broadly striped linen tablecloth

Big white slipware platters

*A pitcher of fresh lemonade (2 cups fresh lemon juice, 1 1/2 cups sugar, 6 cups water,
2 sliced lemons for floating, 4 mint sprigs for deliciousness—optional)*

An Amish basket for the cornbread

AMERICAN BUFFET

Meatloaf Plus with Spicy Gremolata Stuffing and
Tomato Sauce with Fresh Marjoram

Chicken Fingers and Deep-fried Herbs with Sweet Potato Dip

Heavenly Cornbread

A Huge Pile of Grilled Shrimp

The Ultimate Potato Salad with Juniper and Buttermilk

Succotash for Oscar

Chocolate Shortcake with Strawberries, Milk Chocolate Puddle,
and Mascarpone

Banana Bourbon Cream Pie with Macadamia Crust

THE IDEAL AMERICAN MEAL

For some reason, a buffet suits the American way of life and style of entertaining better than any other. It's the opposite of formal or stuffy and allows the freedom of choice, which every American I know, relishes. It also kindly accepts the coming and going of the television watching, sports-playing, unstoppable conversationalists *(We'll be right there . . .)* who rule this land—not to mention the inevitable tangle of children and big dogs, and probably six extra friends dropping by at the last minute. All the food here is at least as good at room temperature as it is served hot, which eliminates the stress of all the food having to be ready at the same time, and all the people being ready to eat it at the same time.

This particular American buffet demonstrates a certain generosity, including an outsized meat-loaf and lashings of sauce, a huge pile of shrimp, potato salad with everything, cornbread that's a meal in itself, and the creamiest, fruitiest, most chocolat-y and diet-defying desserts on the planet. It's a slightly out-of-control meal that might daunt someone from a more austere nation, but it suits the rambunctious American spirit to a tee.

MEATLOAF PLUS WITH SPICY GREMOLATA STUFFING AND TOMATO SAUCE WITH FRESH MARJORAM

Serves 12 to 16

Client: "We want the meal to be American, you know, but really, really . . . SPECIAL."

Me: "How about meatloaf? That's American, and we can make it special."

Client: "Well, it needs to be absolutely fa-a-abulous . . . and different."

Me: "We'll add all sorts of interesting herbs and extra seasonings and stuff it with gremolata and breadcrumbs, and wrap it with hickory smoked bacon and serve it with our tomato sauce with fresh marjoram, and it'll be the best you've ever tasted."

Client: "But will it be REALLY SPECIAL?"

This is the kind of conversation we occasionally have at the catering company. *No amount of words, however you string them together, are worth one bite of the real thing, because once tasted it's a fait accompli.*

In making this "reallyreallyspecial" meatloaf, the only thing to remember is not to mash the mixture to death. Handle it as gently as possible while trying to mix all the ingredients together evenly. Crumble the meat into the bowl when you start. If the meat isn't stone cold, it will be more receptive to mixing without overworking. There are a lot of ingredients here but they're well balanced—do try it my way before making any changes.

THE MEATLOAF

- 2 pounds ground beef
- 1 pound ground pork
- 1 pound ground turkey
- 2 medium onions, finely diced
- 2 cups finely grated carrots
- 1 heaping tablespoon minced garlic
- 1/2 cup heavy cream
- 3 extra-large eggs
- 1/2 cup packed fresh breadcrumbs (see Note)
- 1 heaping tablespoon minced fresh rosemary
- 2 generous tablespoons Dijon mustard
- 2 tablespoons kosher salt
- 2 teaspoons freshly ground black pepper
- 1/4 cup Heckers or King Arthur all-purpose flour

These are the shortest instructions in the book: Put all the ingredients for the meatloaf in a big bowl and mix together well. Set the mixture aside and make the stuffing.

THE SPICY GREMOLATA STUFFING

- 3 tablespoons olive oil
- 2 medium onions, finely diced
- 3 cups fresh breadcrumbs (see Note)
- 1/2 cup minced Italian parsley leaves, including a few crunchy stems
- 2 extra-large eggs

3   strips lemon zest, minced

2   strips orange zest, minced

4   garlic cloves, minced

2   teaspoons kosher salt

$1/2$ teaspoon hot red pepper flakes

1   pound thinly sliced hickory-smoked bacon, for assembly

    Tomato Sauce with Fresh Marjoram (recipe follows)

Put the olive oil and onions in a medium sauté pan over medium heat and cook about 15 minutes, or until translucent. Then in a

large bowl, mix the onions with the rest of the ingredients for the gremolata stuffing.

Position a rack in the middle of the oven and preheat to 375°F.

To assemble, lay 6 slices of bacon in a rectangle on a sheet pan. With dampened hands arrange half the meatloaf mixture over the bacon in a 15- by 5-inch oval. Knuckle a shallow 12- by 3-inch depression to hold the stuffing, pile it in, and form a smooth shape. Cover with the rest of the meatloaf mixture, then pat firmly to seal the edges, and press upward to make a nice high shape. Drape the meatloaf with more slices of edge-to-edge bacon, (see page 3). Bake for 35 minutes, then turn the heat up to 450°F for 15 minutes to brown the surface. Remove from the oven and let the meatloaf rest for at least 15 minutes. Serve hot or at room temperature, with the Tomato Sauce with Fresh Marjoram. You can choose whether to present the meatloaf whole on a big platter, or slice it in 3/4-inch-thick pieces in the kitchen.

Note: For fresh breadcrumbs, you need a food processor (which makes them easily) or a blender (which requires patience as the cubes of bread tend to get stuck). Using day-old crustless peasant bread, cut the bread into 1-inch cubes and process in batches. Five cups of cubes make about 3 1/2 cups breadcrumbs.

TOMATO SAUCE WITH FRESH MARJORAM

This is a fabulous sauce with that mysterious marjoram flavor, and it goes particularly well with the meatloaf.

1/4 cup extra virgin olive oil

1 medium onion, diced

3 garlic cloves, sliced

1 1/2 teaspoons kosher salt

Two 28-ounce cans plum tomatoes in juice

2 tablespoons chopped fresh marjoram leaves (or 2 teaspoons dried)

1/2 teaspoon freshly ground black pepper

2 tablespoons aged sherry vinegar (see Resources, page 211)

Put the olive oil, onion, garlic, and salt in a medium, nonreactive saucepan over medium heat and sauté gently for 10 to 15 minutes, or until the onion is translucent. Drain the tomatoes, reserving the juice; trim off the stem end of each tomato, then chop the tomatoes into 1/2-inch pieces. Add the tomatoes, their juice, 1 tablespoon of the fresh marjoram (or 1 teaspoon of the dried), and the pepper. Then COVER and adjust the heat to a simmer. Cook for 20 minutes, then UNCOVER and cook for 30 minutes, or until the sauce has reduced and thickened. You may need to stop cooking sooner, or cook it down more, depending on your definition of "medium" heat—this is what cooking is all about. Stir in the second tablespoon of marjoram (or the 1 teaspoon dried) and the sherry vinegar. This sauce can be held, covered, in the fridge for 2 days or frozen for up to 6 weeks.

CHICKEN FINGERS AND DEEP-FRIED HERBS WITH SWEET POTATO DIP
Makes 25 pieces

This is a simple dish, however wonderful, and no amount of fancy names (*goujons de poulet frites*) or indications of an ancient heritage can disguise that fact. It's just—and I use the word "just" with hesitation—chicken, marinated in buttermilk, herbs, and spices,

coated with seasoned panko—Japanese breadcrumbs—see Resources, page 211, and fried in corn oil; the deep-fried herbs add a touch of urbanity. The chipotle- and honey-spiked sweet potato dip we serve it with is another mind-boggling conversation stopper.

One evening at the catering company we had a meeting with a couple to see if we were the right people to cater their wedding. We all became so engrossed in talk of flowers, invitations, and music that we totally forgot the hors d'oeuvres we had planned to tempt them with. Before they left, they asked to see the kitchen, so we gave them a tour and then (feeling totally stupid) found all their beautiful food sitting on fancy trays. They nibbled on everything and seemed to like it, then as they were leaving, Juan, the sous chef, walked by with a big tray of hot chicken fingers for another party. Everyone's eyes lit up and, unbidden, our hands reached out; the tray was appropriated, and we made quite a dent. I asked poor Juan, who was busy cooking replacement fingers, to unpack the dip so they could try that too, and then—after working their way through a quart—a Southern theme was decided upon, so they could legitimately build the whole wedding around our irresistible chicken fingers and sweet potato dip.

THE CHICKEN

- 5 pounds skinless, boneless chicken breast, trimmed of fat and connective tissue
- 1 1/2 cups buttermilk
- 3 extra-large eggs
- 1 tablespoon crushed garlic
- 1 teaspoon paprika
- 1 1/2 tablespoons dried oregano
- 1 tablespoon kosher salt
- 1 1/2 teaspoons hot red pepper flakes

Cut each chicken breast into 2 1/2-ounce strips of even thickness and set aside in a large bowl.

In another bowl, mix together the buttermilk, eggs, garlic, paprika, oregano, salt, and pepper flakes and pour over the chicken. Mix well, cover, and put in the fridge for 2 hours, or overnight.

THE COATING

- 3 1/2 cups panko breadcrumbs (see Resources, page 211)
- 1 1/2 cups Heckers or King Arthur all-purpose flour
- 1 tablespoon kosher salt
- 2 teaspoons paprika
- 1 teaspoon freshly ground black pepper
  Vegetable oil for frying

Mix the panko, flour, salt, paprika, and pepper together in a shallow tray.

Coat the chicken pieces and set aside. Put a wide sauté pan over medium heat, add oil to 1/3-inch depth, and heat for about 5 minutes.

Turn up the heat to high, then add as many chicken pieces as will fit in the pan without crowding— the oil should come halfway up the chicken—and sauté for 3 to 4 minutes on each side, or until golden brown and crisp. Drain on a rack and serve hot with Deep-fried Herbs and Sweet Potato Dip (recipes follow).

THE SWEET POTATO DIP

3 pounds sweet potatoes, peeled and cut into 1 $^1/_2$-inch even chunks

4 tablespoons ($^1/_2$ stick) unsalted butter

2 tablespoons honey, or to taste

$^1/_2$ teaspoon chipotle chili powder, or to taste (see Resources, page 211)

1 teaspoon kosher salt

$^1/_2$ teaspoon freshly ground black pepper

Put the sweet potatoes in a medium saucepan and cover with cold salted water. Bring to a boil, then reduce the heat to a simmer and cook covered for 15 to 20 minutes, or until a knife pierces the sweet potatoes easily.

These sweet potatoes, and in fact any root vegetable, *must be mashed while they're still very hot or something scientifically disastrous happens and they turn into rubbery lumps that will never mash smoothly.* So drain them and straightaway put the sweet potatoes in an electric mixer fitted with a balloon whisk. Add the butter, honey, chipotle powder, salt, and pepper, and beat to a smooth puree. You could make this mash ahead of time. Cover and

refrigerate for up to 2 days or freeze for up to 6 weeks. To heat, defrost if frozen, then just warm through in a pan over low heat, stirring occasionally. Serve hot in a bowl next to the chicken fingers.

THE DEEP-FRIED HERBS

Cesare Casella, the chef and owner of Beppe restaurant in Manhattan, is the prince of fried herbs. He tucks them into his deep-fried potato wedges and, when there's a lull in service, he tours the restaurant with a fistful of fresh herbs peeking out of the pocket of his chef's whites.

CESARE CASELLA'S TIPS

1 The herbs must be absolutely dry.

2 Never use olive oil to fry them—peanut or other vegetable oils are preferable.

3 Bring 2 inches of oil in a small saucepan to 375°F. on a candy thermometer. Fry sage for about 2 minutes, rosemary and thyme for about 1 $^1/_2$ minutes, and basil for about 1 minute. Whichever herb you're cooking, when it changes color, it should be done.

6 sprigs rosemary

6 stems leafy basil, washed and dried, with any long stems trimmed

Vegetable oil for frying

Fry the herbs without crowding the pan, using Cesare Casella's tips above. Remove them carefully with a slotted spoon and cool on the same rack as the chicken.

HEAVENLY CORNBREAD
Makes one 9- by 9-inch pan
(see photograph, page 155)

You can get by without cornbread, so if you're going to make it at all, why not make it exceptional? I'm a cornbread lover but not necessarily a purist, and I'm perfectly ready to unite many felicitous counterpoints, hot and smoky, sweet and salty, damp and crunchy. I use double-smoked bacon fat in the bottom of the pan, but when vegetarians are on the horizon, corn oil is perfectly fine. This cornbread is irresistible both hot out of the oven AND at room temperature.

2 tablespoons double-smoked or regular bacon fat (or substitute corn oil)

THE DRY INGREDIENTS

1 cup Heckers or King Arthur all-purpose flour

3/4 cup uncooked instant polenta

5 tablespoons sugar

1 tablespoon plus 1/2 teaspoon baking powder

2 teaspoons kosher salt

1/2 teaspoon freshly ground black pepper

1/4 teaspoon hot red pepper flakes

THE WET INGREDIENTS

1 cup buttermilk

2 tablespoons vegetable oil

1 extra-large egg

THE CHUNKY STUFF

2 cups fresh sweet corn kernels, uncooked

1 tablespoon jalapeño pepper, seeded and diced small (or to taste)

1 red Holland pepper, grilled (see Note) and diced small, to make 1/3 cup packed

Position a rack at the top of the oven and preheat to 350°F. Put a pan and the 2 tablespoons of bacon fat or oil in the oven to heat until the batter is ready.

In a large bowl, whisk together the dry ingredients. In another bowl, whisk together the wet ingredients, then stir in the chunky stuff.

Quickly fold the wet ingredients into the dry and scrape into the hot pan. Level the batter and bake for 30 minutes, or until a toothpick comes out clean. Cool for 15 minutes, then turn out of the pan and reverse back onto a rack to finish cooling.

Try not to cut the cornbread too far in advance, as the edges will dry out. If you need to cut it earlier, put it back in its original square shape, then separate it just before serving time.

Note: If you have a gas stove, to "grill" a single pepper, rest it over a high flame on the stovetop, turning it with tongs until the whole pepper is black, about 10 minutes. Put it in a baggie for 10 minutes to steam, then peel off the black skin, de-seed, and dice the flesh.

A HUGE PILE OF GRILLED SHRIMP

Serves 10

How utterly appealing does that sound? Everyone likes the "huge" thing, as on the whole no one can ever have too much shrimp, and the idea of a "pile" is so generous and easygoing—so American. No silver salvers, just an excess of shellfish bathed in olive oil, garlic, hot pepper flakes, lemon zest, and minced rosemary.

<table>
<tr><td>1/3</td><td>cup olive oil</td></tr>
<tr><td>2</td><td>garlic cloves, crushed</td></tr>
<tr><td>1/2</td><td>teaspoon hot red pepper flakes</td></tr>
<tr><td>1/2</td><td>teaspoon minced lemon zest</td></tr>
<tr><td>1</td><td>tablespoon fresh lemon juice</td></tr>
<tr><td>2</td><td>tablespoons minced fresh rosemary leaves</td></tr>
<tr><td>1</td><td>tablespoon kosher salt</td></tr>
<tr><td>1 1/2</td><td>teaspoons paprika</td></tr>
<tr><td>3</td><td>pounds shrimp (approximately 50), peeled and deveined, with tails left on</td></tr>
</table>

Mix the olive oil, garlic, red pepper flakes, lemon zest, lemon juice, rosemary, salt, and paprika together in a large bowl, then toss the shrimp through the mixture. Set aside for 1/2 hour or so, covered in the refrigerator.

Preheat the grill or broiler for 15 minutes or until very hot. Dab some crumpled-up paper towels in olive oil and, using tongs, rub the bars of the grill with the paper to prevent sticking. Cook the shrimp for about 2 minutes on each side depending on the size. You could serve these grilled shrimp as a wonderful first course for a dinner party, on a bed of arugula dressed with aged balsamic vinegar and extra virgin olive oil.

THE ULTIMATE POTATO SALAD WITH JUNIPER AND BUTTERMILK

Serves 10 to 12

I was born in England, and when you started from London, it was very easy to spend a weekend in another country altogether.

In the sixties and seventies, travel was quick and cheap. The future husband and I—yes, we were living in sin—would wake before dawn (or forgo sleep altogether, as it was usually when the nightclubs closed that a trip seemed like a good idea), we'd grab our passports and a change of clothes, and hop on over to Europe, in all its infinite variety.

On Monday morning, no one would think it particularly exciting that we'd been to the flea market Paris or eaten churros at a street fair in Barcelona.

I first tasted warm potato salad with juniper berries and melting onions at an inn in the Black Forest and just loved it, so when I tried to think of something to perk up normal potato salad . . . there were the juniper berries, lurking in the shadow of a big tree.

2 1/2   pounds small red or white potatoes

1   teaspoon kosher salt, plus more for cooking the potatoes

2   tablespoons Grey Poupon country brown mustard

3   tablespoons white wine vinegar

1   tablespoon chopped juniper berries

1/4   cup buttermilk

1/2   teaspoon freshly ground black pepper

1/2   cup golden olive oil, such as Filippo Berio brand

1/2   cup minced Italian parsley

1/2   cup minced scallions (using the white and the green parts)

Try to find really small firm potatoes, and pick ones out that are all the same size. Line a sheet pan with paper towels and set aside.

Cut the potatoes into even, wedge-shaped quarters; cover with well-salted cold water and bring to a gentle simmer. Don't let them boil furiously or they'll break apart. Cook until a knife penetrates a potato wedge with a little resistance—they shouldn't be mushy. Drain and briefly rinse with cold water to stop the cooking. Spread out the potatoes on the paper towels to air dry.

To make the dressing, stir the mustard, vinegar, juniper berries, buttermilk, salt, and pepper together in a medium bowl. Slowly whisk in the olive oil until the dressing is creamy.

In a large bowl, toss the slightly warm pota-toes with three-quarters of the dressing. Cover and set aside for up to 24 hours. Fifteen minutes to 1 hour before serving, add the remaining dressing and fold in the parsley and scallions.

SUCCOTASH FOR OSCAR
Serves 10

I first came up with this version of succotash for a dinner party featured in Rena Sindi's book on entertaining, *Be My Guest: Theme Party Savoir-Faire*. It was the most wild and beautiful evening imaginable—especially when you consider the theme was "Spring," a supposedly mild season. The party was hosted by Oscar de la Renta in conjunction with Saks Fifth Avenue.

There were six tables of ten, each with different centerpieces, ranging from star anise-filled glass vases coiled around with giant amber necklaces, to full-blown lacy pink and snow white peonies as pure as hopeful debutantes (or hopefully pure).

The tables themselves were swathed in bouf-fant chartreuse net, topped with white eyelet cotton squares (a pretty hint of spring there), and the white ballroom chairs had two pink satin bows tied to their backs. The food had to look good on the plate, taste good, and pho-tograph well. Because each component was cooked separately and cooled quickly to set the color, the final dish looked tremendously fresh and clean. Just as we had planned.

3 cups fresh sweet corn kernels

2 teaspoons kosher salt, plus more for cooking the corn and haricots verts

1 pound haricot verts, trimmed and cut into $^{1}/_{2}$-inch diagonal pieces

1 firm red Holland pepper

$^{1}/_{2}$ cup loosely packed basil leaves

3 tablespoons extra virgin olive oil

$^{1}/_{2}$ teaspoon smoked paprika

1 teaspoon freshly ground black pepper

1 to 2 bunches fresh basil, for decoration

Put the kernels in a small saucepan of lightly salted water. Cook over medium heat until al dente, 5 to 7 minutes, then drain and run under cold water to stop the cooking. Scatter the kernels on a paper towel–lined sheet pan.

Cook the haricots verts in the same way as the sweet corn but for only 3 to 5 minutes.

Cut down each side of the red pepper making 4 square slabs. Cut each slab into $^{1}/_{4}$-inch strips, maintaining the square shape, then cut diagonally into $^{1}/_{2}$-inch pieces. Set aside.

Stack the basil leaves 5 to 10 at a time and roll them into a lengthways cylinder. With a sharp knife, cut across the cylinder, slicing the basil into thin shreds.

TO ASSEMBLE

Put everything into a big mixing bowl with the olive oil, smoked paprika, salt, and pepper. Stir and taste for seasoning. Chill for an hour before serving. A big bouquet of basil stuck in the side of the serving bowl looks very dashing.

CHOCOLATE SHORTCAKE WITH STRAWBERRIES, MILK CHOCOLATE PUDDLE, AND MASCARPONE

Makes 12 shortcakes

This sounds difficult, but it's really not. In fact, it can all be prepared a day before, baked, and then assembled two hours before your party. You could requisition a friend to come early and stack it all together for you; it's such a beautiful thing, how could they complain?

SO, there are four pieces to the puzzle.

THE MILK CHOCOLATE PUDDLE

1 cup heavy cream

10 ounces milk chocolate, chopped

Put the cream in a small saucepan and set it over medium heat. When tiny bubbles appear around the edge, turn off the heat and tip in the chocolate. Shake the pan to submerge the chocolate, wait 1 minute, and then stir to combine. Pour into a plastic container (to make it easier to soften later in the microwave) and set aside.

THE STRAWBERRIES

32 ounces (8 cups) strawberries

2 to 4 tablespoons sugar, depending on the sweetness of the berries

Wash, dry, and hull the strawberries. Then cut them in halves or quarters depending on their size. Mix with the sugar and set aside, leave covered in the fridge for at least 1 hour, and preferably overnight.

THE SHORTCAKE

3 cups Heckers or King Arthur all-purpose flour

6 tablespoons cocoa (see Resources, page 211)

1/3 cup plus 1 tablespoon sugar

2 teaspoons baking powder

1 teaspoon baking soda

1 teaspoon kosher salt

8 tablespoons (1 stick) unsalted butter, cut in 1/2-inch dice and chilled

2 cups heavy cream

2 teaspoons pure vanilla extract

1 extra-large egg white for the glaze

Position a rack in the top of the oven and preheat to 425°F. (Do give the oven time to reach this high temperature as these shortcakes are rich, and like the Montgolfiers, need a blast of hot air to rise properly.)

Put the dry ingredients and the butter in a food processor and give 10 short pulses to mix. Tip into a WIDE SHALLOW BOWL. Pour the cream and vanilla over the cocoa mixture. Using a large fork, quickly and lightly mix the wet into the dry. When the ingredients are just combined, leave to rest for 5 minutes, then lightly gather into a ragged mass, tip out onto a floured surface and lightly shape, then roll into a horizontal 9- by 12-inch rectangle.

Brush with the egg white and sprinkle on the 1 tablespoon of sugar. Trim the edges straight with a long, thin sharp knife. Then cut the dough into 12 squares making 2 equal cuts across and 3 down (or cut into twelve 3-inch circles with a cookie cutter). Put the shortcakes on a baking sheet about 1 inch apart and bake for 15 to 20 minutes, or until just firm. Remove from the oven and set aside to cool on a rack. Split in half horizontally while still warm and set the tops back on the bases.

THE MASCARPONE

Two 8-ounce containers mascarpone

This is an Italian cream cheese with a sexy smooth-as-satin texture and a tangy flavor that balances the great richness. It's available in the refrigerated section of large supermarkets and in Italian groceries.

TO ASSEMBLE

Arrange all the shortcake bases on a platter, spoon on 2 or 3 tablespoons of strawberries with their juice, and then spoon on 2 tablespoons of the mascarpone. Place the top shortcake half on, squashing down lightly so the mascarpone oozes out. Spoon more strawberries and mascarpone on top, then set aside for up to half an hour. Soften the ganache in the microwave on the defrost setting, until it has a thick pouring consistency, then spoon it over the shortcakes just before serving. Top with a juice-soaked strawberry.

BANANA BOURBON CREAM PIE WITH MACADAMIA CRUST
Serves 10 to 12

If, like me, you worship at the altar of the dessert goddess, you'll go mad for this pie, surely one of her favorites too. The original recipe comes from *The New Basics Cookbook* by Julee Rosso and Sheila Lukins, who generously said I could adapt it and adopt it for my own. This pie makes strong men moan and women weep, so watch out.

THE CRUST

- 2 cups macadamia nuts
- 1 cup flaked unsweetened coconut
- 1/4 cup packed light brown sugar
- 2 extra-large egg whites

    Vegetable oil for the pan

Position a rack in the middle of the oven and preheat to 350°F.

Pulse the macadamias and coconut together to medium fine in a food processor. Tip the mixture into a bowl, and using your fingers, thoroughly blend in the sugar. Using an electric mixer, beat the egg whites until stiff but not dry then fold them in.

I make this pie in a 12-inch round skillet from Analon (see Resources, page 211). It works beautifully, as it is heavy and has a low, sloping side that makes the removal of the crust very easy. The pan can go in a 350°F oven with impunity.

Tip the crust mixture into the pan and pat it out evenly to cover the whole pan. (I never think there will be enough, but there is.) Make sure the edges are uniformly thick. With your thumb, push the crust at the edge firmly in and slightly up above the rim, then pat down with your index finger as you go around to make a strong edge.

Bake for 15 to 20 minutes, or until golden. Set aside in the pan to cool completely (wrapping the handle). If you're not using the crust until the next day, loosen it from the pan using a long narrow spatula but leave it in the pan, cover with plastic wrap, and refrigerate.

THE CUSTARD

4 tablespoons bourbon, whiskey, or rum

1 packet Knox powdered gelatin

4 extra-large egg yolks

2/3 cup sugar

1/2 teaspoon kosher salt

2 tablespoons cornstarch

1 1/2 cups whole milk

2 tablespoons unsalted butter, at room temperature

2 teaspoons pure vanilla extract

Put the alcohol in a small pan, then sprinkle on the gelatin and set aside to soften. In a medium saucepan, FIRST stir together the egg yolks, sugar, and salt, THEN sift in the cornstarch and whisk together well. Whisk in the milk, and when smooth, add the butter. Cook over medium heat until thick and bubbling, about 5 minutes, then take it off the heat straightaway or the cornstarch will overcook and lose its thickening power. Melt the softened gelatin over low heat; it mustn't boil or the setting property will diminish, but it must be completely liquid. Pour the gelatin into the custard, add the vanilla extract and mix well. Cover with plastic wrap pressed onto the surface, then refrigerate for 4 hours, or ideally, overnight.

THE ASSEMBLY

1/2 cup heavy cream

4 perfectly ripe bananas with little brown spots on the skin

1/4 cup sweetened shredded coconut, toasted at 350°F for 5 to 10 minutes, or grated semisweet chocolate, for decoration

Remove the plastic wrap from the custard and whisk to loosen. (If it's very stiff, give it a whirl in the food processor.) In an electric mixer with the balloon whisk, beat the heavy cream fairly stiffly and fold into the custard. Cut the bananas down the middle and then into 1/4-inch slices and fold them in as well. Carefully slide the pie crust from its pan. Put it on the plate you'll be using and spread the banana custard into the crust. Smooth the top evenly and refrigerate until serving time, then scatter on the coconut or chocolate.

THE WAY TO GO

Choosing a menu for a dinner party that allows me to sit and eat with my friends and avoid any last-minute cooking is my ideal. I'm prepared to work the night before and up to an hour or so prior to everyone's arrival, but that's IT. Having a catering company has taught me a lot about dinner parties, and most people can't believe how much can be done ahead, and left in a low oven or on a low heat until serving time. I am perfectly happy to leave a roast to relax for an hour; the meat won't be boiling hot, but the plate and the sauce or gravy can be. ***When everything tastes wonderful, you have lots of leeway.***

In this chapter, there's food for each season and ideas to make the cooking of it easier. I've focused on the kind of real food people eat at home rather than in restaurants, where the chef gets to flambé wildly one minute before the food is due at the table.

The trick is beautiful presentation, not overly-worked food. I've been to dinners where the host or hostess has gone WAY overboard, trying to make three complicated courses where one must be hot and one must be cold (but not too cold, you understand). Interesting stories at the table are interrupted by cries for help in the kitchen and anxious frowns appear when a layered soufflé collapses too fast under the weight of its own importance. So take it easy, and when you have a special need to show off, you can do it with different wines for every course ***and gorgeous flowers.***

DINNER PARTY MANTRA: PERFECT INGREDIENTS, SIMPLY COOKED, ON PRETTY PLATES

DINNER PARTY POLICY

1 Plan for as little last minute cooking as you can possibly manage.

2 Tell your guests the time frame. You could say, "Come any time from six-thirty; we'll be sitting down at eight." Make sure they have your phone number so they can call if they'll be late. If you live out of cell phone range, let your guests know that when you invite them, and tell them you will start without them so they can be lost in peace.

3 Allow enough time to get yourself dressed in a civilized manner—i.e., not a whirling dervish—before your guests arrive.

4 If you're having more people than usual, test the table setting a couple of days before to make sure that everything fits. You might do without bread plates if space is tight, or put the dessert spoons and forks above the plate. Check that you have enough chairs and they fit around the table comfortably.

5 If your dinner party is to introduce new friends, relatives, or potential husbands and wives, seating them correctly is imperative. It's better to chew on your pencil beforehand and make a seating plan than to have everyone staring at you expectantly, their hand on the back of the nearest chair—then foist the job on your *glowering spouse.*

6 Have enough plates, glasses, and cutlery so you NEVER have to wash spoons or bread plates to use for dessert.

7 Buy a small, sturdy collapsible coat rack (from Hold Everything, see Resources page 211). Coats left in a pile on the bed become creased; can be taken in error; and keys, credit cards, and cell phones slide right out of the pockets.

8 Guests often turn up with flowers even though a beautiful potted plant is a little kinder on the host. Rather than dumping the flowers in the sink (totally in your way) have ready a large and small vase full of water, just in case, so you can pop them in and *bring the flowers out, as if by magic.*

9 Steel yourself to breeze over any breakage or spillage. It's always an accident, and you can unleash your primal scream when the guests have gone.

10 Don't fuss over unexpected vegetarians or people with wheat allergies, etc. They'll work it out. As you know, there's always going to be someone who doesn't eat something. Do them a favor and don't comment. Don't even look at that expensive lobster languishing on their plate—it doesn't exist.

11 Put together dessert plates and any serving utensils so there's no last minute searching for a knife or a ladle.

12 Put together the coffee cups, spoons, milk, sugar, and sweeteners, and time your coffee machine so the coffee is freshly brewed when you need it.

13 At the end of the night, when guests ask if they can help clean up, do be explicit. "Absolutely not" or "That would be great" are good. "Oh, no, well . . . you shouldn't, really," is bad. If you do decide to ask for help, set a mental fifteen-minute deadline—anything more becomes a chore.

Shrimp, Fennel, and Orange Soup with Crostini and Rouille

Butterflied Leg of Lamb Roasted with Ginger and Garlic
Tomatoes Stuffed with Rice, Pine Nuts, and Fresh Oregano
Steamed Peas and Sugar Snap Peas

Raspberry Frangipane Pie with Almond Whipped Cream

SHRIMP, FENNEL, AND ORANGE SOUP WITH CROSTINI AND ROUILLE

Serves 8

This soup is one of those dangerous appetite ruiners that prompt guests—as I'm trying to remove their soup bowls—to forget their dinner party manners, clutch onto the bowl and brazenly ask for second helpings. The crunchy, fresh fennel fronds scattered in just before serving play wonderfully with the sweet and hot rouille. And the rouille with the Grilled Garlic Crostini floats on top of the soup like a little red raft.

If any of your guests have a problem with shellfish, you can make this soup without the shrimp and it will still taste sublime—just set a helping of soup aside before you add the shrimp. Look for fennel bulbs with light green fronds in the center.

THE SOUP

1 pound shrimp, peeled and deveined, cut across into $1/4$-inch slices

1 tablespoon extra virgin olive oil

2 teaspoons kosher salt

1 teaspoon freshly ground black pepper

4 tablespoons ($1/2$ stick) unsalted butter

1 pound juicy fennel, trimmed and chopped whole, including the heart

1 medium yellow onion, diced medium

3 strips orange zest

3 cups homemade or College Inn chicken stock

1 $1/2$ cups orange juice (with no pulp)

$1/2$ cup minced fennel fronds and tender stalks, wrapped and refrigerated

Grilled Garlic Crostini
(see recipe, page 86)

Rouille (recipe follows)

Heat the soup, add the shrimp, float a crostini spread with rouille on top or pass the crostini and the rouille separately. Remove the minced fennel fronds from the fridge and scatter them over the soup.

Note: Covering the pan creates a mini pressure-cooker so the heart of the fennel will cook through quickly.

CROSTINI AND ROUILLE

THE GRILLED GARLIC CROSTINI
(see recipe, page 86)

THE ROUILLE

1   red Holland pepper

1   slice country bread, 1/2-inch thick, crusts removed

2   garlic cloves, chopped

1/4   teaspoon hot red pepper flakes

1/4   teaspoon smoked paprika (see Resources, page 211)

1/2   teaspoon kosher salt

6   tablespoons extra virgin olive oil
   Freshly ground black pepper

In a medium bowl, mix the shrimp with the olive oil, 1 teaspoon of the salt, and 1/2 teaspoon of the pepper. Cover with plastic wrap and refrigerate. Put the butter in a medium saucepan over low heat; when it's melted, add the chopped fennel bulb, onion, orange zest, the remaining teaspoon of the salt, and the remaining 1/2 teaspoon of the pepper. Stir to coat everything with butter, cover the pan (see Note), and cook for 20 minutes, stirring occasionally and adjusting the heat so nothing browns. Add the chicken stock and orange juice and simmer, covered, for 20 minutes. Puree in batches in a blender and set aside.

A couple of hours before your guests arrive, put a sauté pan over high heat, add the shrimp, stir-fry quickly for about 2 minutes or until the shrimp is just cooked. Set aside.

If you have a gas stove, the easiest way to cook a single red pepper is to lay it on a high flame and just keep turning it with tongs until it's very charred and blackened, then put it in a plastic or Ziploc bag to steam for at least 10 minutes. When the pepper has cooled,

remove the peel and seeds and chop the flesh roughly. Dip the bread in water to dampen it a little and lightly squeeze dry. If you have a mortar and pestle, put in the red pepper, garlic, hot red pepper flakes, paprika, and salt, and pound together to a paste. Continuing to pound with the pestle, gradually adding the bread torn into 1-inch chunks while you drizzle in the olive oil; the mixture will become as thick as mayonnaise. Season to taste with black pepper. Remove from the mortar and set aside.

If you don't have a mortar and pestle, you can use a food processor—just put everything in and puree. It's easier but not such a satisfyingly ancient method, and the texture will be more uniformly smooth. Spread each crostini with rouille and float on the hot soup.

If you prefer, slice and bake the whole loaf and bring the crostini to the table in a basket with a double batch of rouille in a separate bowl. Everyone can spread their own and float it on the soup, or not.

THE ROUILLE CAPER STORY When I was catering in Manhattan—while living and cooking all the food an hour and ten minutes away in North Salem— various problems presented themselves. The main ones were being stuck in traffic, and therefore late, or leaving something vital miles behind.

Kim (the boyfriend, partner person) and I erred on the side of caution and often arrived so early that we'd end up going shopping and spending all the money we were about to make. As for leaving anything behind—I became a checklist lunatic and usually had to be frog-marched out of the house still licking my pencil.

I became so anxious about forgetting a critical element of the meal that I sometimes made Kim stop the car so I could rifle through all my careful packing, turning it upside down, looking for the possibly truant basil butter . . . or some such treasure that I was POSITIVE had been left on the kitchen table. I could only really relax at the halfway mark, as then all you could do was press on.

One Sunday, I was driving in alone, with a meal for thirty people based around a glorious cioppino, or fish stew. I knew every element was perfect, especially the rouille, the garlicky red pepper sauce that would complete the dish. I had found beautiful purple-skinned garlic and shiny, heavy red peppers; I had driven rather obsessively to the next town for a loaf of dense country bread and had used really good olive oil.

I arrived with time to spare, lugged the food in a tub up to the client's kitchen, and she watched as I unpacked. We chatted brightly about the upcoming meal, then there was a pause as I transferred the cioppino and she asked, "Where's the rouille?" I glanced down into the plastic tub. *I would rather have seen a nest of tarantulas than what I DID see—which was nothing.*

"Oh, silly me . . . (sorry, but I could NOT admit to having left it behind) it's in the back of the car. I'll just get this all ready, then I'll nip and fetch it."

Meanwhile, I was having what my doctor son calls an M.I., or myocardial infarction—i.e., a heart attack. I took the stairs three at a time, hit the street running, and burst into a mangy deli around the corner. I picked up a dusty jar of roasted peppers, a shriveled head of garlic with a tangle of green shoots waving out of the top, a loaf of squishy white bread, and a bottle of corn oil.

Fervently praying *(I think I might have offered up my dog)* that a good friend who lived two doors down was in, and had a food processor. Both prayers answered. Miranda had been in the Peace Corps and was always good in a crisis. She opened the jar of peppers and started tearing the bread out of the bag. I was picking at the garlic with shaking hands, trying to get the skin off . . . it was in horrible shape. We jammed everything into the food processor, tipped in salt and some of her hot pepper flakes to try and perk up the flavor. As I poured oil in through the top of the machine, Miranda yelled, "Only pulse, or you'll ruin it!"

"Ruin what???" I wailed.

We stared at the pink product of our panic. It had a faint whiff of garlic and was good and spicy. We pronounced it not bad . . . considering.

I think I was back in the other kitchen in fourteen minutes. "Really," I said, "I don't know how you keep a car in the city. The parking people are so slow."

The next morning, the client left a message. "Darling, you really outdid yourself. We all agreed it was better than in Marseilles, and Bill is begging for the rouille recipe . . . he said he'd never had one quite like yours. *Divine. Much love.*"

BUTTERFLIED LEG OF LAMB ROASTED WITH GINGER AND GARLIC

Serves 8 (see photograph, page 172)

If you've read the Lamb in the Pine Trees story, (next page), you might wonder what I was up to with this wanton embellishment of a perfectly good leg of lamb. But as you'll see, fresh ginger and lamb when roasted together create the most luscious flavor. Ask the butcher to butterfly the leg (removing the bone and opening the leg to make a flat piece of meat) and then back home spend five minutes with a sharp knife trimming up his or her handiwork. You will divide the leg into individual sections, following the muscles.

There's a bit of waste, but you end up with pure meat and a judicious amount of fat, which helps baste the roasting meat, plus the end result is so much easier to carve than a whole leg with bones in it.

6 tablespoons extra virgin olive oil

2 tablespoons minced rosemary

4 tablespoons finely minced fresh ginger

1 tablespoon minced garlic

4 teaspoons kosher salt, divided

2 teaspoons freshly ground black pepper

One 7-pound leg of lamb, butterflied

Put the oil in a small pan over medium heat. When hot add the rosemary, ginger, garlic, 3 teaspoons of the salt, and pepper. Sauté for 1 minute, then remove from the heat. Allow the mixture to cool, then rub the paste into the lamb. Cover loosely and refrigerate for at least 4 and up to 24 hours.

Take the lamb out of the fridge 2 hours before cooking. Position a rack in the upper third of the oven and preheat to 400°F.

Set a large nonstick saucepan over high heat and heat the pan for 2 minutes. Keeping the heat high, sear the lamb on both sides in batches. Scrape any scraps of rosemary and ginger in the saucepan onto the seared meat after each batch.

Arrange the lamb on a sheet pan and put in the oven to roast. Start checking the smaller pieces for doneness after 10 minutes. The largest piece will take about 20 minutes. If you have a meat thermometer, use it now. My thermometer broke about 6 years ago (memo from the school of antique cooking habits) so I use a metal trussing skewer. I stick the skewer into the center of the meat, wait 5 seconds, then touch the skewer to my cheek. If the metal is warm, the meat is done. This trick caused an uproar of consternation in the catering office, prompting a chorus of "How warms?" . . . so maybe a meat thermometer is the way to go. Aim for 350°F.

Allow the lamb to rest for 20 minutes. Thinly slice and serve warm or at room temperature.

LAMB IN THE PINE TREES STORY When I was nineteen, I went on holiday with the future husband and friends, to Crête. He'd heard about a five-hour hike, over mountains, through forests, down a winding gorge, and so to the sea. Being youngish and optimistic, we'd set off early, planning to have lunch at a local taverna on the beach, famous for its stuffed tomatoes.

I remember we were all very jolly for the first couple of hours. The path was shaded, finches darted through the branches, and aromatic pine needles crunched under our feet. Even when we emerged from the trees and started climbing the FIRST mountain, we were still innocently marvelling at the views and dear little flowering plants.

As the sun rose, our spirits sank. Far below us we could see the verdant gorge that was our route to the stuffed tomatoes, but we could have seen it better with binoculars. We slogged on, becoming rather quiet and blistered. I'll skip past the accusatory, finger-pointing moment as sweat dribbled into our eyes and the future husband took it on the chin for having misrepresented this arid march so completely.

Finally, our heads hot and aching and our thighs trembling like Olympic long distance runners—or so I imagined—we entered the silent shade of tall pine trees and gratefully came upon the sparkling mountain stream that had been responsible for the gorge in the first place. We drank from the stream and soaked our sorry feet.

On stopping to regroup, another problem surfaced. We were wolfishly hungry; we were lightheaded and had stabbing pains from our middle-class stomachs that were not used to being denied. Feeble exhortations about "when the going gets tough" fell on irritable ears.

We plodded on, having, we calculated, three more hours to go. I was a few yards ahead of the others and was just thinking, "If I never see another pinecone, that would be absolutely fabulous," when I got a whiff of something cooking. I dismissed it as delusional but stopped in my tracks anyway. My friend Philip came up behind and said, "Is it only me, or do you smell lamb roasting over an open fire?" Well, that was EXACTLY what I'd thought, and to hear the words out loud made the idea seem possible. But how could this be? We were slap-bang out in the middle of nowhere. We all scrambled down the path and rounded a corner to find a beatifically smiling old man sitting with his dog outside a vine-covered hut. He was turning not one, but TWO legs of lamb over a wood fire on a makeshift spit. We were transfixed and could only goggle at the glistening meat—our manners and *kalisperas* gone out the window.

Being English, it was absolutely wrong to indicate that we would like to eat all his lamb right away—even for money, which we were feverishly rustling in our pockets. Having a shred of a classical education didn't help, *as I considered that this was probably Zeus on a prank, and if we ate anything at all, we'd be turned into bleating sheep and have to wander around the mountains for eternity.*

The dear old man, being so splendidly Greek, insisted we sit and eat with him. He conjured up two bottles of retsina—idiosyncratic Greek wine—and a rusty corkscrew with half a handle. The future husband scored mightily by producing his "Pride of Zurich" Swiss Army knife, which included six useful bits and bobs including a state-of-the-art corkscrew. We saw our host's eyes virtually pop out of his head as the knife's every trick was revealed until it looked like a shiny red and silver porcupine. It was offered in exchange for the quintessential lamb and wine, since money was out of the question. Apparently there was equity in the deal, and we parted with much handshaking, backslapping, and bashfully received kisses.

The dog had found the bones that were thrown deep into the trees, the man had the knife, and we had tasted lamb that couldn't have been improved upon, under any circumstances, in any country.

TOMATOES STUFFED WITH RICE, PINE NUTS, AND FRESH OREGANO
Serves 8

This is one of my dearest recipes, as before I made some fine adjustments, I followed the instructions written out by my son Sam when he was ten. (See Sam, page 202)

Sam and I were on the Greek island of Paxos, having a terrible time on vacation. At the bottom of my barrel of ideas for entertaining him, I insisted he write postcards to everyone he had ever known. He'd left his father till last and was out of postcards. Since his dad was a must, Sam asked for one of my Greek recipe postcards plucked from the stand outside the local post office. The postcards simply explained the making of baklava, moussaka, stuffed tomatoes, and avgolemono. I agreed, as long as Sam copied out the recipe for the stuffed tomatoes so I could stick it in my book. Twenty-two years later, it's still there; a chocolate thumbprint and a splash of pink beet juice share the page with his carefully penciled words, which include his own precocious aside—"Maybe could be made with peppers too?"

What a good boy—and we still call them "Postcard Stuffed Tomatoes."

3/4 cup short grain brown rice

1 tablespoon plus 1 teaspoon kosher salt

1/4 cup Greek or extra virgin olive oil, plus more for drizzling

1 large onion, diced

8 firm, ripe tomatoes on the vine, cut off the vine, leaving a little stalk

2 garlic cloves, minced

1 tablespoon minced fresh oregano (or 2 teaspoons dried)

1/2 teaspoon freshly ground black pepper

1/3 cup pine nuts

Position a rack in the upper third of the oven and preheat to 350°F. Oil a 13- by 9-inch heavy metal, ceramic, or glass baking dish and set aside.

Put the rice and 1 tablespoon of the salt in a medium saucepan, cover with cold water by 2 inches, and bring to a simmer over medium heat. Cook approximately 30 minutes, until the rice is still a little chewy. Drain and reserve.

While the rice is cooking, put the olive oil in a medium heavy-based saucepan and set over medium heat. Add the onion, and gently sauté until translucent, 5 to 7 minutes. Cut a good slice off the tomatoes at the stalk end for the lid and shave a little slice off the base so the tomatoes stand straight; set each top next to its tomato. Use a teaspoon to scoop the pulp out into a small bowl, chop the pulp, and add it to the onions along with the accumulated tomato juices and the remaining teaspoon salt, the garlic, oregano, and pepper. Cook briskly for 5 minutes. Add the rice and stir for 3 minutes, or until most of the liquid is absorbed; set aside to cool. Stir in the pine nuts, then fill the tomatoes (making sure not to pack down too tightly), piling the mixture over the rim. Press each tomato lid down on top, and place the stuffed tomatoes 1 inch apart in the baking dish. If there is any extra rice mixture, spoon it around the tomatoes. The dish can be brought to this point the day before, covered, and refrigerated. When you're ready to bake the tomatoes, drizzle with a little extra olive oil and bake for 45 minutes to 1 hour, depending on the size of the tomatoes, adding 10 minutes if they are cold from the fridge.

These look most authentic if the tomato skin is slightly blackened on the top. If necessary, turn the oven up to 450°F for the last 5 to 10 minutes. The good news is that these tomatoes are just as *katapliktiko* (unspeakably fabulous) warm or at room temperature, so you could bake them earlier in the day if you need space in the oven. Cover with plastic wrap while the tomatoes are still just a little warm. The condensation that forms will keep them from drying out.

STEAMED PEAS AND SUGAR SNAP PEAS

Serves 8

You can cook just one or the other, but I like the combination of shapes.

One   16-ounce package frozen baby sweet peas

1/2   pound sugar snap peas

2   teaspoons extra virgin olive oil

1/2   teaspoon kosher salt

1/4   teaspoon freshly ground black pepper

Bring a medium pot of lightly salted water to a boil, add the frozen sweet peas, cook for about 2 minutes, drain, and set aside. Grasp the tip of the stalk end of each sugar snap pea and pull down, removing the string along the spine. Cook the sugar snap peas in the same way as the sweet peas, but for 3 minutes, or until still crunchy. Drain and immediately run the peas under cold water to stop the cooking. Tip them into a bowl with crumpled-up paper towel on the bottom, pour on the sweet peas, and set aside to drain well. Remove the paper towel, add the olive oil, salt, and pepper and stir to mix. To heat, either microwave at a low level until hot or put in a heavy-based saucepan with 1 tablespoon water over low heat; cover and steam for 5 minutes.

RASPBERRY FRANGIPANE PIE WITH ALMOND WHIPPED CREAM

Serves 8

This is the recipe I have struggled with most in the whole book. I first had it at a hedonistic brunch buffet in Arizona with Husband #2. Then I came back to New York and made it successfully MANY times.

Got divorced, didn't make it for ten years, and suddenly, when I wanted to, couldn't make it right for the life of me. Finally I gave up and

invented a new pie with a layer of nutty filling. *And guess what. It's better than the old.*

Pie might sound too everyday for a dinner party, but I think it's great. One day at the catering company, a posse of power fashionistas was coming for lunch to talk about events during Fashion Week in Manhattan. I thought it unlikely that anyone would eat dessert, and I just offered one of these pies as a token. Only one person took a slice but then went into such eye-rolling paroxysms of delight, that soon everyone had some, and then seconds, and then it was all gone. They ate all the cream too.

If you haven't made pastry before, this is an ideal time to start, as when the shell is painted with egg white and dusted with sugar and the pie itself baked to a crunchy golden vision, you'll be glad you made the effort. It's so delicious and, I think, impossible to begrudge any time spent in the making.

THE PASTRY

To make the crust, follow the instructions for the pastry in the recipe for the Crostata (on page 120) up to the point where the pastry crumbs have rested for 5 minutes. Compress the crumbs quickly and firmly into an oval shape, then pinch the middle together and form 2 separate discs inside the plastic bag. Put the dough in the fridge for at least 2 hours, or overnight. It can also be wrapped airtight and frozen for up to 2 months. Label clearly, or you might grab it for a savory dish forgetting about the sugar.

THE FRANGIPANE

1/2 cup sliced or slivered almonds

1/3 cup sugar

2 extra-large egg yolks

1/2 cup heavy cream

2 tablespoons all-purpose flour

1 tablespoon whiskey, cognac, or rum (optional)

1 teaspoon vanilla

1 teaspoon pure almond extract

3 boxes (18 ounces) sweet red raspberries

Put all the ingredients, except the raspberries, in the bowl of a food processor and blend for 30 seconds. Scrape around the base with a rubber spatula and blend for another 30 seconds. Transfer the almond cream into a small bowl, cover, and set aside.

Remove the pastry from the fridge and leave at room temperature for about 15 to 20 minutes, or until just pliable but still cool. Roll one of the discs out to a 13-inch circle and—making sure it's centered—drape the pastry over a 10-inch pie dish, preferably of black metal.

Pour in the almond cream and scatter over the raspberries. Using a pastry brush, brush the egg white on the pastry rim around the edge. Roll out the other pastry disc and drape it over the raspberries. Press the pastry layers together, then using scissors, trim to 1/2 inch. Brush the whole top with the egg white and

casually crimp the edges, pressing them together so they stay put, then dredge the pie with the last tablespoon of sugar.

Take a small sharp knife and make 5 or 6 cuts in the crust so the steam can escape. I forgot the cuts once. The steam blew the top crust up into a dome and the raspberries turned into a seedy red swamp, so the cuts are pretty important.

Put the pie in the freezer, unwrapped, for 30 minutes. Position a rack in the middle of the oven and preheat to 425°F.

Bake the pie for 25 minutes, adjust the heat to 350°F, and bake for another 20 minutes. If the crust is getting too dark, lay a sheet of aluminum foil loosely on top of the pie. Remove the pie from the oven and cool for at least 45 minutes before serving with the almond whipped cream or with vanilla or chocolate (!) ice cream.

THE ALMOND WHIPPED CREAM

- 1 cup heavy cream
- 3/4 teaspoon pure almond extract
- 1/2 teaspoon pure vanilla extract
- 1 tablespoon sugar

Using an electric mixer, beat all the ingredients at medium speed (high speed makes the cream too fluffy, and full of air) until soft peaks form. Serve in a beautiful bowl, add a silver ladle, and pass with the raspberry pie.

Salad of Steamed Asparagus with Mixed Herbs and Preserved Lemons
Toasted Pita with Green Herb Butter

Oven-Roasted Halibut in Charmoula Marinade
Couscous with Dates and Pine Nuts
Carrot Salad with Rose Water and Cilantro

Double Almond Cake
Cardamom-Poached Apricots and Greek Yogurt

MAKE PRESERVED LEMONS TODAY

A reminder, just in case you are breezing through this book anytime between the months of February and April.

If you have half an hour—once you get back from the shops with everything you need—you could get these lemons preserving away on a shelf, so that when you want to make this particular summer menu, there they'll be. There's no quantifying how much better yours will be than any bought in a shop, if you can even find them—maybe eighteen million times better. They're related to normal preserved lemons but have a few unlikely ingredients . . . and they're spectacular. You must use kosher salt, not regular salt.

PRESERVED LEMONS

Three 16-ounce preserving jars
3 teaspoons pink peppercorns
3 teaspoons black peppercorns
3 teaspoons white peppercorns
1 teaspoon whole cloves
1 teaspoon whole coriander seeds
6 to 8 firm lemons
3 bay leaves
3 large cloves garlic, unpeeled
9 tablespoons kosher salt
1 1/2 cups fresh lemon juice (approximately 9 lemons)

Sterilize the jars you're going to pack the lemons in (see Note). In a small bowl, mix together the pink, black, and white peppercorns, the whole cloves, and the coriander and set aside. Scrub and dry the lemons and cut them in vertical quarters. As they're cut, start packing them in the jars and add the mixed spices, bay leaves, garlic, and the kosher salt as you go. When the jars are full, pour 1/2 cup lemon juice in each, then fill with cold water. Close the jars, shake well, then top up with water to just below the rim and close tightly. The next day, tighten the lids. You'll notice as the skin becomes saturated with the brine it will lose its clear yellow color; and in 6 weeks, the lemons will be ready. Once opened, the lemons will keep unrefrigerated for several months—just keep them under the brine and out of direct sunlight.

Note: To sterilize the jars, place the jars and lids in a large saucepan and cover with water. Bring to a boil, and boil for 20 minutes, topping up with boiling water as needed. *(Boil, boil, boil.)* Remove with tongs and air-dry.

SALAD OF STEAMED ASPARAGUS WITH MIXED HERBS AND PRESERVED LEMONS
Serves 8

I have a passion for asparagus and whole wheat bread. As a child in England, I loved asparagus spears rolled in thin, buttered brown bread cut in two-inch lengths, and eaten at tea-

time. At seven years of age, I considered this the very pinnacle of civilization. Even venturing into the realm of exotic North African herbs and spices, as in this menu, doesn't preclude the urge to pair the two again.

THE ASPARAGUS AND ITS DRESSING

4 pounds asparagus

1/4 cup plus 1/2 teaspoon kosher salt

2 preserved lemon quarters (see preceding recipe)

1 clove garlic, crushed

1/4 teaspoon hot red pepper flakes

1/4 cup extra virgin olive oil

Trim the woody ends off the asparagus, cut the stalks diagonally into 1-inch pieces, and set aside. Fill a medium bowl halfway with ice water and set aside. Bring 2 quarts of water to a boil in a large saucepan, add 1/4 cup of the kosher salt—the cooking time is so fast you need a lot of salt to make any difference—then add the asparagus and cook for about 1 1/2 minutes, until still quite crunchy (see Note). Drain and dump the asparagus into the ice water to stop the cooking. Swirl around with a wooden spoon for 30 seconds, drain again, pat dry, and set aside.

To make the dressing, cut the flesh off the preserved lemon, removing most of the pith, and squeeze the salty juice into a small bowl; discard the pulp. Take the peel, lay it skin side down; cut into 1/2-inch strips, then across into

fine diagonal splinters. Add the peel, garlic, pepper, and 1/2 teaspoon salt to the lemon juice, then whisk in the olive oil. Cover and set aside. Wait to toss the asparagus with the dressing until you're ready for assembly.

Note: If any asparagus spears are noticeably thicker, cook them in a separate pan, a little bit longer than the thinner spears.

THE GREEN HERB SALAD AND ITS DRESSING

- 1 bunch fresh mint (if any leaves are very large, tear in half)
- 1 bunch fresh basil
- 1 bunch fresh tarragon
- 1 bunch fresh cilantro
- 1 bunch fresh Italian parsley
- 1 tablespoon extra virgin olive oil
- 2 whole fresh lemons
- 1 teaspoon fleur de sel (see Resources, page 211) or kosher salt
- 1/2 teaspoon freshly ground black pepper

You want 1 packed cup of assorted herb leaves, so pick off as many leaves as you need, then wash and dry them well. Wrap in damp paper towels, and put them in a Ziploc bag in the fridge.

Cut the peel and any white pith off the fresh lemons. Using a small, sharp knife, cut first down one side of the connecting membrane and then down the other side to remove the first lemon segment and place it in a bowl. Then—now you have room to maneuver— cut down along the second piece of membrane, turn the blade under and ease the lemon segment off the third membrane. Continue with the whole lemon, discarding any seeds, cut each segment into 3 pieces and set aside. Move on to the next lemon.

TO ASSEMBLE

When you put this salad together, toss the asparagus in its dressing and pile in the middle of each first course plate, where it can wait till you top it with the herbs. Not to cause undue stress, but once the herb salad is mixed, it must be eaten right away; otherwise, it will wilt. When you have everyone sitting down, toss the herbs quickly and gently with the olive oil and then the lemon segments, divide onto the asparagus, and sprinkle with the salt and grind on the pepper.

TOASTED PITA WITH GREEN HERB BUTTER
Serves 8

1 to 2   bunches perky Italian parsley

1   package large whole wheat or white pita bread with a pocket (the small size pita is too thick)

Green Herb Butter (see recipe, page 117), at room temperature

Position a rack at the top of the oven and preheat to 400°F.

Trim the parsley stems and put the bunch in a glass half filled with water. Open a small plastic bag, slip it over the parsley, pull the bag tight at the base, and put the whole thing in the fridge. This way the parsley will stay perfectly fresh until you need it.

Cut around the perimeter of each pita with scissors, then carefully pull apart. Spread the two halves each with a thin layer of herb butter, then sandwich them firmly together again. Cut into large, irregular wedges and lay edge to edge in a single layer on an unlined, ungreased sheet pan and bake for 7 to 10 minutes, or until the edges turn golden and the bread is crisp. Serve in a basket lined with a bed of the Italian parsley so you don't get butter all over your napkins.

ABBY STORY Charmoula isn't a concoction one might happen upon by experimentation, as the ingredients are precisely balanced. This recipe came to us from Abby, a passionate chef from Morocco, who was with the catering company for a few months. He allowed himself no restraints in the kitchen and operated in a ballet of perpetual motion—stirring a tagine, chopping mint, dusting with smoked paprika, and plunging his hands into bowls of oiled lamb shanks marinating in aromatic herbs. Then—as the formalities of a French kitchen weren't for him—wiping those hands on his chest or just continuing to stir and chop, leaving a trail of greasy knives and slippery saucepan handles in his wake. He was such a fabulous cook that we just followed him around with a damp cloth and did the best we could.

One day I came into the kitchen and something was different. Abby was standing still and measuring rather carefully. It was an unusual sight, so I was compelled to stand by his side and see what was going on. "Is charmoula," he said, with a fond smile. "My mother, she teach me and she VERY good cook. I always make exact the same."

I leapt for pen and paper, as Abby's food was wildly changeable, and up until that moment there had been no possibility of harnessing him to a single version of anything. Maybe this was the one time I could get him to relay some of his genius and give me a RECIPE (for heaven's sake). He did, and this is it, though I've reduced the quantity, which was probably *enough for a whole village.*

OVEN-ROASTED HALIBUT IN CHARMOULA MARINADE
Serves 8

THE CHARMOULA MARINADE
Makes about 1 $1/2$ cups

One-and-a-half cups is more than you'll need, but it will last for at least two weeks refrigerated and is wonderful rubbed on chicken, lamb shanks or chops, steak, or salmon—so get some friends over and use it up.

- $1/2$ cup chopped cilantro leaves
- $1/2$ cup chopped Italian parsley leaves
- $1/2$ cup fresh lemon juice
- 2 preserved lemon quarters (see page 179)
- 3 teaspoons paprika
- $2/3$ teaspoon cayenne pepper
- 1 $1/2$ teaspoons Ras el Hanout (recipe follows)
- 1 $1/2$ teaspoons cumin
- 1 $1/2$ teaspoons kosher salt
- 2 garlic cloves, crushed
- $1/2$ cup extra virgin olive oil

To make the marinade, mix all the ingredients together in a medium bowl.

- Eight 8-ounce center-cut halibut fillets
- $1/2$ cup Charmoula Marinade

Put the halibut in a large bowl. Pour on the marinade and gently turn to coat the fish on all sides. Cover with plastic wrap and refrigerate for at least 1 hour.

Position a rack in the middle of the oven and preheat to 350°F. Line a sheet pan with parchment paper.

Place the halibut fillets 2 inches apart on the sheet pan and bake for about 10 minutes, or until just cooked through. Serve hot, warm, or at room temperature. The beauty of this marinade is its magical ability to saturate food with flavor at any temperature.

RAS EL HANOUT
Makes $1/4$ cup

I've heard that ras el hanout can be made from thirty spices and herbs, but these seven seem perfectly fine to me. PLEASE take the time to make this—it's an irreplaceable ingredient in North African dishes, and in addition to flavoring the Charmoula Marinade, it can be added to couscous or tagines.

- **3** bay leaves
- 1 $1/2$ teaspoons dried thyme
- 1 $1/2$ teaspoons white peppercorns
- 1 $1/2$ tablespoons crumbled whole nutmeg (see Note)
- 1 cinnamon stick, broken in pieces, OR
- 1 $1/2$ teaspoons ground cinnamon
- 1 $1/2$ teaspoons whole cloves
- 1 $1/2$ teaspoons ground ginger

Combine everything in a spice mill and blend until fine. Rub through a sieve and store airtight. Ras el hanout will stay potent for 6 weeks.

Note: To crumble nutmeg, wrap a paper towel around 2 or 3 whole nutmegs and hit them sharply a couple of times with a small, heavy saucepan.

COUSCOUS WITH DATES AND PINE NUTS
Serves 8

I know this may not sound like the easiest thing in the world to make, but it actually is (especially with quick-cooking couscous). Of course, "easy" is only easy if you have couscous, preserved lemon, olive oil, dates, and pine nuts on hand in the kitchen cabinets or fridge. The only thing you have to buy especially would be the fresh cilantro.

One   10-ounce box plain couscous, preferably Near East brand

2   tablespoons extra virgin olive oil

2   teaspoons kosher salt, divided

1/4   of a preserved lemon (see recipe, page 179)

6   dates, pitted, cut down the middle then across into 1/4-inch pieces

1/4   cup pine nuts

1/4   teaspoon freshly ground black pepper

1/2   teaspoon ground cumin

1/4   cup minced fresh cilantro

Put the couscous in a wide bowl with the olive oil and 1 teaspoon of the salt. Pour on 2 cups of boiling water. Stir to mix and leave covered with a cloth (or plastic wrap) for 5 minutes to absorb the water.

Use a fork to fluff the couscous; if there are any lumps, break them up by rubbing them gently between the palms of your hands. Pull the flesh off the peel of the preserved lemon and squeeze the salty juice over the couscous, discarding the pulp. Lay the peel flat and run a knife horizontally just under the pith to remove it; dice the remaining peel in 1/8-inch pieces and scatter over the couscous with the remaining teaspoon salt, the dates, pine nuts, pepper, cumin, and cilantro and toss together. This dish can be made up to 6 hours before the meal, covered, and set aside, out of the fridge. The couscous can be served at room temperature or, to serve hot, put it in a strainer over 2 inches of simmering water, covered—a paper towel is fine—and heat for about 7 minutes.

CARROT SALAD WITH ROSE WATER AND CILANTRO
Serves 8

This combination isn't written in stone. Lisa, one of the event planners who worked at the catering company, had to almost leave the room at any mention of rose water, she hated it so much. And in reality there are plenty of people who don't like cilantro, but if you've made preserved lemons, don't skip by this recipe; it can be made without the rose water, and with parsley or dill instead of cilantro.

2 1/2 pounds carrots (see Note)

1 tablespoon and 1 teaspoon kosher salt

1 1/4 preserved lemons (see recipe, page 179)

2 tablespoons fresh lemon juice

2 tablespoons extra virgin olive oil

1/4 teaspoon freshly ground black pepper

1 teaspoon rose water (optional)

1 1/2 tablespoons minced cilantro leaves

1 1/2 tablespoons minced Italian parsley

Line a sheet pan with paper towels and set aside.

Bring a medium saucepan half filled with water to a boil. Add the carrots and 1 tablespoon of the salt. Bring back to a simmer, and after about 6 minutes, start hooking out pieces to test for doneness; if necessary, allow another minute or two, and keep testing—it's the only way to catch them just right.

While the carrots are cooking, start the marinade; you're going to toss the carrots in it while they're still warm. Pull the flesh off the peel of the preserved lemon and squeeze any salty juice into a medium bowl; discard the pulp. Lay the peel flat and run a knife horizontally under the pith to remove it; cut the remaining lemon peel into 1/2-inch strips, then into very fine splinters called "julienne." In the bowl, add the peel, the fresh lemon juice, olive oil, the remaining 1 teaspoon salt, pepper, rose water, cilantro, and parsley; whisk together and set aside. When the carrots are cooked, drain and tip onto the sheet pan to cool for 5 minutes, then toss with the marinade. Just before serving, toss again to coat with the glistening, scented oil.

Note: Peel then cut the carrots diagonally in 3/4-inch chunks, and as much all the same size as possible. They'll look prettier and cook more evenly this way. *Imagine how impossible it would be to achieve uniformly al dente pasta if the penne varied in size . . .* and you're aiming for al dente carrots. Big, older carrots can cook more quickly, while carrots bought in bunches with greens still attached can take longer.

RUBY LOVES CARROTS

THE GIGANTIC LADIES' LUNCH CAKE STORY The first time I made this cake it was as an experiment to develop the quintessential almond cake, and to see if I could find any short-cuts. The reason for this research was that I had commissioned myself—too cheap to pay anyone else—to make eighty-five of these little beauties for a gigantic ladies' lunch at Lincoln Center. (You understand the number of ladies was gigantic, not the ladies themselves.)

When you're attempting a scientific practice session, it's a really good idea to go it alone. You can make notes, adjust quantities, and check for doneness in peace. On this particular evening, my kitchen was full of interesting, chatty people and what with all the badinage, it was a miracle that I got anything finished at all. The recipe I was following became substantially altered as I distractedly added ingredients and invented procedures. When the third batch was voted delectable, I knew secretly that I had lost track of its evolution . . . I was forced to frisk the minds of my friends, asking, "But what did you see me do?" and "How much almond extract? . . . sugar?. . . one cup or two?" We put our heads together and the recipe was eventually written in stone. The eighty-five cakes were a success, deliciously damp inside and crunchy outside. We served them with poached apricots, crème fraîche, and a jaunty sprig of rosemary. At the lunch I sat two away from Claudia Fleming, the paragon of pastry chefs. She took one bite and put down her fork. I started to feel dizzy with anxiety and asked what the problem was. Phew . . . just an iron will on a low-carb diet.

DOUBLE ALMOND CAKE WITH CARDAMOM-POACHED APRICOTS AND GREEK YOGURT

Makes one 9-inch cake

THE DRY INGREDIENTS

1 1/4 cups blanched sliced almonds, toasted at 350°F for 10 minutes, divided

2 cups Heckers or King Arthur all-purpose flour

2 cups sugar

1 teaspoon baking powder

1/2 teaspoon baking soda

1 teaspoon kosher salt

THE WET INGREDIENTS

12 tablespoons (1 1/2 sticks) unsalted butter, melted

2 extra-large eggs

1 cup buttermilk

1/2 teaspoon pure almond extract

1 teaspoon pure vanilla extract

Position a rack in the middle of the oven and preheat to 350°F. Grease a 9-inch cake pan.

Throw 1/4 cup of the toasted almonds into the greased pan and turn the pan to coat the inside with the nuts. In a wide bowl, sift together the flour, sugar, baking powder, baking soda, and salt, and toss through 1/2 cup of the almonds. In a medium, deep bowl, whisk together the butter, eggs, buttermilk, almond extract, and vanilla. Pour over the dry ingredients, and fold in gently with a rubber spatula.

Scrape the batter into the prepared pan and scatter the last 1/2 cup of almonds around the edge. (If you put too many almonds in the middle they'll sink.)

This cake is fragile in the oven, so don't slam the oven door if you open it once it has started to rise. Bake for 55 minutes, or until a toothpick inserted in the center comes out clean, and the edge of the cake is shrinking away from the pan. Cool completely in the pan.

THE CARDAMOM-POACHED APRICOTS

1 pound dried apricots

1 quart (4 cups) orange juice, strained of pulp

2 teaspoons cardamom seeds (see Resources, page 211)

3 strips lemon zest

3 strips orange zest

Put everything in a medium, heavy-based, non-reactive saucepan and bring to a SLOW simmer over medium heat. Cover and cook gently for 30 minutes, then uncover, and cook for another 30 minutes, until the apricots are plumped up but not mushy. Set aside to cool, then transfer them to a container and leave overnight in the fridge. I find the apricots (in fact, any poached fruit) need 24 hours to settle into their juice and to become properly chilled.

THE GREEK YOGURT

Lebne is the real name for this heavenly, cold, thick cream. Because you use lowfat yogurt and drain it for twenty-four hours, somehow it's rich yet light. If it's too sharp for you, you could add a teaspoon of sugar (or honey), but I love the contrast of the sweet cake, crunchy with almonds, the scented juicy apricots, and this creamy, tart, authentically "Take-Me-to-the-Casbah" yogurt.

1   quart plain lowfat yogurt

Pinch of kosher salt

Scatter the salt on the yogurt in its quart container and stir to incorporate. Pour the yogurt into a cheesecloth or kitchen towel–lined strainer and set over a bowl deep enough to hold up to 2 cups of liquid under the strainer. Flip the ends of the cloth over to cover and leave refrigerated for 24 hours. When you come to use the yogurt, it will be very thick.

Just turn the drained yogurt out onto a plate in one movement (pull off the cheese cloth if it comes with it), and you'll notice a delicate pattern of lines on the surface from the cloth.

To serve, either spoon the apricots into individual dishes with the cake and the yogurt, or bring everything to the table and do it there. Anthony Bourdain, the author of *Kitchen Confidential,* and his wife, Nancy, were at my house for dinner one night. They were as fascinating and gregarious as usual, but Tony really came into his own when I put out this cake with the apricots and yogurt and asked him to make it all happen.

He became a windmill of activity, slicing the cake, spooning the apricots, tapping out the yogurt, and passing the plates like there was no tomorrow. Guests, and especially guests who cook, never mind helping and always love being asked to get involved.

Frisée with Stilton and Crisp Apples
Walnut Dijon Vinaigrette

Beef with Barolo, Wild Mushrooms, and Orange
Celery Root Mash
Roasted Carrots and Rutabaga

Thin Chocolate Tart with Mint and Hot Red Pepper Syrup

FRISÉE WITH STILTON AND CRISP APPLES

Serves 8

This salad has all the usual suspects, but why not give people something easy and delicious as a first course? Look for sprightly, pale frisée with a good heart. It's annoying to spend a fortune on frisée and then have to trim away half of it because it's a bit flabby. I use Braeburn apples. They're tart but perfumed and add a wonderful, slightly sweet foil to the bitter frisée and the pungent Stilton.

- 10 handfuls frisée, about 3 to 5 heads
- Eight 1/2- to 1-ounce slices Stilton
- 2 unpeeled Braeburn apples, sliced thin (as close to the time of serving as possible to avoid oxidization)

Trim away any dark leaves and cut the frisée into bite-size pieces. Soak in iced water for 5 minutes, spin dry, pack in a couple of Ziploc bags, and refrigerate until you're ready to assemble the salad.

WALNUT DIJON VINAIGRETTE

Makes about 1 cup

- 1 clove garlic, minced
- 1 tablespoon Dijon mustard
- 3 tablespoons apple cider vinegar
- 1/2 teaspoon kosher salt
- 1/2 teaspoon freshly ground black pepper
- 1/2 cup extra virgin olive oil
- 2 tablespoons finely chopped Italian parsley
- 1/3 cup walnut halves, minced

Put the garlic, mustard, vinegar, salt, and pepper in a small bowl and stir to mix. Slowly whisk in the olive oil to form an emulsion, and set aside.

To serve, add the parsley and walnuts to the vinaigrette and fold through; toss the frisée and the apple slices with the vinaigrette, and divide them evenly between the plates. Lay a slice of Stilton on top.

THE PRESENT STORY When I first started cooking, it was through the inspiration of Elizabeth David's cookbooks. They suited my temperament, as I was often more impassioned than academic when it came to instructions, and frying something in "a good lump of butter" sounded just about right to me. Her books—piled next to my bed—were read like novels rather than taken to the kitchen, and I would dream about downy purple figs, or scallops swimming in fennel-scented cream. Often, it was the idea of a dish that gripped me rather than the actual recipe, which could prove to be open to interpretation.

Elizabeth David opened her kitchen shop in London's Pimlico not long after I started cooking. I would go there and hang around, pretending I was trying to decide what to buy and covertly watch her. What I really wanted was for all the other customers to evaporate so I could sidle up and have a little discussion about food. Mrs. David was elegant and aloof and would never talk if there were other people around; but I was young and brave and once we were alone, I asked questions about her recipes that amused her, so she indulged me.

One rainy night, I was walking up the dark street toward her shop just to look in the window and thought it had to be open, as there was such a golden glow coming through the glass and reflecting on the wet sidewalk.

The window proved to be full of a new shipment from the south of France. It displayed the most beautiful casseroles: round ones for beef, oval for game, and low circular ones (each with a little round lid) for tripe; there were bowls of every size and generous serving dishes. All had been washed with a soft yellow glaze, which caused the radiance. Strands of the straw they had been packed in littered the shelves and made the earthenware even more out of place on a dark, wet, swinging-sixties London street. *I literally pressed my nose to the glass and basked in the virtual Provençal sun.*

The next day was my birthday, and I went back to buy something. I didn't know what it would be, but I remember relishing the decision. The shop was empty, and Mrs. David was in the back somewhere (I could hear tissue paper rustling—or maybe it was more straw). She suddenly swept out, carrying some empty wooden crates. I told her about the glow the night before and of my determination to buy a present for myself. Maybe she could advise . . . she put the crates down, reached into the window, and handed me a round casserole. "This should be useful," she said. I took it and fitted my fingers into the three depressions on the handles made by the potter's fingertips. I lifted the lid carefully, as the knob was rather small, and stared inside, imagining a simmering daube. I LOVED it and reached for my purse, but she patted my shoulder and said, *"Happy birthday, my dear". . . and it was.*

BEEF WITH BAROLO, WILD MUSHROOMS, AND ORANGE

Serves 8 to 10

Vegetable oil for sautéing

3   large onions, cut into $^3/_4$-inch dice

5   stalks of celery, cut diagonally into $^1/_2$-inch-thick slices

6   garlic cloves, crushed

Three   3-inch strips orange zest (removed with a potato peeler or small knife)

1 $^1/_2$ cups Heckers or King Arthur all-purpose flour

1   tablespoon kosher salt

1 $^1/_2$ teaspoons freshly ground black pepper

3 $^1/_2$ pounds well-marbled beef chuck steak, at room temperature (see Note), trimmed of fat and cut into 1 $^1/_2$-inch cubes

2   cups (or one 15-ounce can) crushed tomatoes

2   cups full-bodied Barolo wine

1   Knorr beef bouillon cube

2   bay leaves

1   tablespoon herbes de Provence (see Resources, page 211)

2   ounces dried porcini mushrooms, soaked in 1 $^1/_2$ cups warm water until soft

Position a rack in the lower third of the oven and preheat to 300°F.

Put 2 tablespoons of vegetable oil in a heavy saucepan over medium-high heat, add the onions, celery, garlic, and orange zest and sauté until wilted and well caramelized, about 10 minutes. Remove with a slotted spoon to a large bowl and set aside. Put 3 tablespoons of vegetable oil in the same saucepan and set it over high heat. While the oil is heating, put the flour, salt, and pepper in a plastic bag and throw in half of the cubed beef. Hold the bag closed at the top and shake to coat the cubes with seasoned flour. Pick the cubes out of the flour and pat them to remove any large clumps of flour, then sauté them in the hot oil for 1 ^{1}/2 minutes on each side, turning with tongs until they are well browned. While they're browning, shake the rest of the beef cubes to coat with flour, then when the first ones are finished, remove them with a slotted spoon to the bowl with the vegetables and sauté the rest, adding more oil as needed. Discard the remaining seasoned flour.

Lower the heat and tip the vegetables and the first batch of the sautéed beef back in on top of the beef in the saucepan. Add the crushed tomatoes, wine, bouillon cube, bay leaves, and herbes de Provence, and stir to mix well, scraping up any brown, crusted areas. Bring to a simmer, stirring occasionally, until the mixture thickens—about 5 minutes.

Line a strainer with paper towels, set it over a small bowl to catch the porcini water, and pour the porcini into the strainer. Gather up the paper towel and gently squeeze to get out most of the water. Rinse the soaked mushrooms, chop them roughly, and add them, along with the porcini water, to the stew. Stir again and transfer the stew to a covered ovenproof casserole.

Put the stew in the oven for 1 ^{1}/2 hours, then test a piece of meat to see if it's tender by trying to cut it with a wooden spoon. If you can't, wait 15 minutes and try again. Depending on the quality of the beef, it could take over 2 hours, so keep calm. Unless you have two ovens, make this stew 1 day ahead, as the roasted carrots and rutabaga need the oven to be at 400°F. Reheat the stew gently in a saucepan on the stove top.

CELERY ROOT MASH
Serves 8

I am in love with celery root. Its craggy exterior gives no indication of the delights that develop once cooked. It is absolutely luscious cut into chunks, parboiled, and roasted (400°F for 40 minutes with olive oil, rosemary, salt, and freshly ground black pepper), but my favorite is this mash. It's feather-light with a haunting flavor that somehow can stand up to the powerful Beef with Barolo (see preceding recipe) and yet is delicate enough to pair with grilled fish or chicken. Usually, celery root is mixed with mashed potatoes, but I think it's much more interesting standing on its own.

In order to break down its rather fibrous texture, mash the celery root in a food processor with lots of pulsing and pushing down of any recalcitrant lumps. Once (by some inconceivable error) I overcooked the celery root and it was a little watery, so after mashing and adding the butter, I put it back in a clean pan over low heat for twenty minutes, stirring occasionally, to dry it out. This step proved to be one of those felicitous moments in the kitchen when near disaster turns to triumph, and the end result was even more delicious than normal, with a creamier texture and stronger flavor. As with duplicate bridge, the same cards played differently can produce both winners and losers.

7 pounds celery root

12 tablespoons (1 1/2 sticks) unsalted butter

1 tablespoon kosher salt

1 teaspoon freshly ground black pepper

3 tablespoons minced Italian parsley

First, bring a medium saucepan of salted water to a boil and keep it simmering. The easiest way to peel a knob of celery root is like a pineapple—just cut off the top and bottom, then stand it upright and cut down around the sides, following the rounded curve. Cut the peeled knob into 1-inch cubes. Put the cubes in a pan and pour on the boiling water to JUST cover. (Don't wash away the flavor with gallons of excess water.) Simmer, covered, for 20 to 30 minutes, or

until a fork (not a knife) pierces the largest pieces easily. Drain well, and while still hot, put in the bowl of a food processor. IF—maybe a distracting phone call?—the celery root inadvertently becomes cold, revert to roasting it in the oven (see above), since it needs to be hot to puree properly.

Add the butter, salt, and pepper and blend, scraping down the sides as needed to create a fairly fine puree. Return the celery root to a clean saucepan and dry out over low heat for 10 minutes, stirring occasionally. The mash can be made the day before, covered, and refrigerated. To reheat, either warm it, covered over a low heat, stirring every now and then, or put it in a covered ovenproof container and heat at 350°F for 20 minutes, or until very hot. Serve with a scattering of parsley over the top.

ROASTED CARROTS AND RUTABAGA
Serves 8

Rutabagas are in the anchovy and sea urchin category of foods, which either evince sparkling eyes or cries of revolt.

I'm in the sparkling department and especially love rutabagas when paired with carrots, to balance their rather bitter, subterranean turnip flavor. You'll often find rutabagas in the store covered with a thin film of white wax. Don't be alarmed, this is just there to keep them fresh.

2 1/2   pounds rutabaga (about 1 large)

1 1/2   pounds carrots, peeled and cut on
the diagonal into 1-inch pieces

1/4   cup golden olive oil, such as
Filippo Berio brand

1   teaspoon kosher salt

1/2   teaspoon freshly ground black pepper

Position a rack in the upper third of the oven and preheat to 400°F.

If you have a knife with a thinner blade than a normal 8-inch chef's knife, use it. It's easier to guide a thinner blade through the rutabaga's dense mass. Slice the top and bottom off the rutabaga with a sharp knife, then standing it on its base, cut down around the sides following the natural curve. Cut the peeled rutabaga into 1-inch slices; lay each slice flat, cut into 1-inch strips, then angle the knife to 45 degrees and cut into 1-inch diagonal cubes.

Put the rutabaga in a medium sauce pan and cover with well-salted water. Bring to a boil and cook for 10 minutes. Drain, then tip into a large bowl and set aside.

Cook the carrots in the same way, but for ONLY 5 minutes after they come to a boil. Drain and add to the rutabagas with the olive oil, salt, and pepper. Toss well and arrange the vegetables in an even layer on an unlined, ungreased sheet pan. Roast for 50 minutes, turning and loosening from the pan with a metal spatula after 25 minutes. Serve hot with a final scattering of salt and a grind of pepper.

THIN CHOCOLATE TART WITH MINT AND HOT PEPPER SYRUP

Serves 8 to 10

As Mrs. Simpson said, "You can't be too thin or too rich." I would agree with reference to this dark little tart.

THE PASTRY

Make half the recipe for the Jam Tart pastry on page 70, and form into a 3/4-inch thick disk. When the dough has been at room temperature for about 15 minutes, roll out to a 12-inch circle, and drape the pastry over a 9 1/2-inch tart pan with a removable base. Starting anywhere, lift the pastry up and ease it down into the corner of the pan, pushing it in with a knuckle then pressing in gently but firmly with your thumb against the vertical side. Run a rolling pin over the top of the pan to cut off the excess pastry. Prick the base 10 times with a fork and put in the freezer, uncovered, for 30 minutes.

Position a rack in the middle of the oven and preheat to 425°F.

Remove the shell from the freezer, line with aluminum foil, tucking it into the corners well, and fill with pie weights or dried beans. Bake for 20 minutes, then remove the foil and bake another 10 to 15 minutes, or until there are no uncooked patches and the pastry is a uniform golden brown. This shell could be baked the day before and left to cool in the

THE CHOCOLATE FILLING

- 8 tablespoons (1 stick) unsalted butter, cut into $1/2$-inch pieces
- 1 cup (8 ounces) chopped Valrhona chocolate
- 1 tablespoon Medaglia d'Oro espresso powder
- 1 tablespoon Heckers or King Arthur all-purpose flour
- 1 tablespoon cocoa (see Resources, page 211)
- $3/4$ teaspoon kosher salt
- 2 extra-large eggs
- $1/2$ cup plus 1 tablespoon sugar
- 2 tablespoons whiskey or bourbon

  Whipped heavy cream, for serving

pan, then filled and baked on the day of the dinner. Just wrap with plastic wrap when the shell is totally cold and don't refrigerate.

Position a rack in the top third of the oven and preheat or adjust the heat to 350°F.

MINT AND HOT RED PEPPER SYRUP
Makes $3/4$ cup

- $1/2$ cup sugar
- $1/2$ cup packed fresh mint leaves, washed well and dried
- $1/4$ teaspoon hot red pepper flakes

The day before you need the syrup, put the sugar and $1/2$ cup of water in a small saucepan over medium heat. Bring to a boil and let bubble away for 2 minutes. Add the mint and pepper flakes, and set aside for 1 hour to infuse. Put the syrup and mint in a blender and blend until smooth. Strain through a sieve and refrigerate until serving time.

Put the butter, chocolate, and espresso powder in a small saucepan on low heat and stir till JUST melted. In a medium bowl, whisk the eggs, sugar and whiskey well; sift on the flour, cocoa, and salt and whisk again. Add the melted chocolate and whisk. Pour the filling into the cooked shell and bake for 10 minutes (for a warm shell), 12 minutes (for a cold shell). The centre will firm as it cools.

To serve, spoon unsweetened whipped cream next to the slice of tart, and then drip the mint syrup off the end of a spoon in beautiful freeform patterns.

Spiced Borscht

Pork Fillet with Juniper and Prunes
Buttered Brussels Sprouts
Polenta with Fresh Sage

Coffee Crème Caramel
Walnut Shortbread

SPICED BORSCHT
Serves 8

I think the only way to serve soup as a first course is in elegant cup-shaped, or antique crystal bowls. When it's offered in wide soup plates with a rim, you have to pour in so much to make the soup plate look full that your guests might be totally full themselves before the main course.

This borscht is such a pretty color you may be deluded into thinking it would taste insipid. In fact, the opposite is true; it's grown up and opinionated, and the flavor just goes on developing till the last mouthful.

3 pounds beets (about 12 medium), divided

2 tablespoons vegetable oil or duck fat

2 medium onions, coarsely chopped

1/2 small green cabbage, shredded

4 garlic cloves, unpeeled

12 cups homemade or College Inn chicken stock, or more if needed

4 whole cloves

2 bay leaves

1 teaspoon hot red pepper flakes

2 tablespoons whole black peppercorns

1 Knorr beef bouillon cube

1 cup sour cream

3 tablespoons aged sherry vinegar (see Resources, page 211)

2 teaspoons kosher salt, or to taste

1 bunch fresh dill, minced, for garnish

Position the rack in the middle of the oven and preheat to 350°F.

Wash the beets, and if they have any leaves, trim them to 1 inch. Put half of the beets (all of a similar size) in a baking dish. Add 1/4 inch of water and cover carefully (to make the dish air-tight) with a double thickness of foil.

¹/2 cup of the sour cream and blend until very smooth. You can either make this soup on the day you serve it, or hold it overnight in the refrigerator. Either way, add the vinegar and salt to taste, when the soup is hot. Use the last ¹/2 cup of the sour cream to swirl on top of the soup, then scatter with fresh dill.

PORK FILLET WITH JUNIPER AND PRUNES
Serves 8

This extraordinary marinade makes an otherwise dull pork fillet taste wonderfully medieval. So much so that I felt compelled to pair it with another ancient ingredient . . . prunes, which, with their chewy sweetness, temper the mouthwatering riot of vinegar, juniper, and bay. The fresh and crunchy Brussels sprouts and polenta—so beautifully creamy and strewn with velvety sage (see following recipes)—make it hard to know where to start when presented with a plateful of all this good stuff.

THE PRUNES

20 plump pitted prunes
2 ¹/2 cups full-bodied red wine
1 tablespoon of sugar

Put the prunes in a small saucepan, add the wine and sugar, and bring to a simmer for 10 minutes over medium heat. Push the prunes under the liquid and set aside, covered, for 24 hours, then drain, reserving the liquid (you'll need ¹/2 cup for the gravy), and

Place the beets in the oven for 1 hour, or until the point of a knife enters easily. When they're cool, peel, roughly dice, and set aside.

Cut the remaining beets into 1-inch chunks. Put the oil in a large, heavy-based saucepan over medium heat; add the beet chunks, onions, cabbage, and garlic. Stir well to coat with oil, then sweat, covered, for 5 minutes, stirring a couple of times. Add the chicken stock, cloves, bay leaves, hot pepper flakes, peppercorns, and the bouillon cube. Cover and bring to a gentle simmer for 1 ¹/4 hours. Strain the mixture, pressing down well on the solids, which you then discard. You should have 8 cups of beet stock. If you're short, add some more chicken stock, and if you have too much liquid, put it back on the stove and reduce to the required amount.

Using the blender (fold a kitchen towel, lay it over the lid of the blender, and hold the lid down firmly . . . JUST IN CASE) puree the reserved cooked beets with the stock, then add

arrange on an oiled sheet pan ready to be
roasted with the pork.

THE MARINADE

2 1/2 cups red wine (a full-bodied Merlot
        or Shiraz)

  1/2 cup red wine vinegar or 1/4 cup aged
        sherry vinegar (see Resources,
        page 211)

  1/2 cup gin

2 peeled shallots, sliced

3 garlic cloves, sliced

2 teaspoons whole coriander seeds

2 teaspoons whole black peppercorns

1 teaspoon kosher salt

1 tablespoon juniper berries, chopped

3 bay leaves

5 sprigs Italian parsley

3 sprigs fresh thyme or 2 teaspoons
   dried thyme

Put all the ingredients for the marinade in a nonreactive pan over medium heat. Cover, bring to a simmer, and cook for 10 minutes. Set aside to infuse and cool.

Take a small garbage bag and a large bowl; open up the bag within the bowl and drape the top of the bag over the rim. Put in the pork, pour in all the marinade, then gather up the plastic and twist it so there's no air left in the bag. This way the marinade will cover all sides of the pork. Leave it in the bowl just in case it leaks, and put in the refrigerator for 24 hours (see Note).

THE PORK

Pork fillets are usually sold in pairs. The two fillets weigh in at about 2 1/2 to 3 pounds, so if you have serious eaters or would like some leftovers, buy two packages of pork (four fillets). Otherwise just buy the largest package of two fillets in the store. The marinade would be sufficient for four fillets.

2 or 4 pork fillets
       Vegetable oil for the sheet pan
2 or 4 teaspoons kosher salt
1 or 2 teaspoons freshly ground black pepper
3 or 5 tablespoons golden olive oil, such as Filippo Berio brand

Position a rack in the middle of the oven and preheat to 350°F.

Take the fillets out of the marinade, reserving 1 cup marinade for the gravy. Set the pork aside for 1 hour to come to room temperature, as you won't be able to brown the meat if it's cold. (At this point you could make the gravy, see below.) Pat the fillets dry with paper towels, and sprinkle with the salt and pepper. Set a wide sauté pan over high heat, add the oil, and when it's very hot, carefully lay in 2 of the fillets using tongs. Sear on all sides until well browned, about 5 minutes. Place the seared fillets on the oiled sheet pan with the prunes. Roast for 15 to 20 minutes, or until a meat thermometer reads 145°F. Remove from the oven and set aside in a warm place to rest for 15 minutes.

THE GRAVY
Makes 3 cups

1/4 cup golden olive oil, such as Filippo Berio brand, divided
1 medium onion, cut in 1/2-inch dice
1 medium carrot, peeled and cut in 1/2-inch dice
2 garlic cloves, sliced
1 teaspoon kosher salt
1 teaspoon freshly ground black pepper
2 1/2 cups chicken stock, homemade or College Inn
1/4 cup Heckers or King Arthur all-purpose flour

Put 2 tablespoons of the oil in a small, heavy saucepan over medium heat. Add the onion, carrot, garlic, salt, and pepper and sauté,

covered, stirring occasionally, for 30 minutes, or until the vegetables are very soft and darkly caramelized. Add the chicken stock, the 1 cup reserved pork marinade, and the ¹/2 cup reserved liquid from the prunes, and cook at a simmer for 30 minutes. Blend the flour with the remaining 2 tablespoons of oil to make a roux, then whisk into the hot liquid to incorporate. Adjust the heat to a simmer and cook for 10 minutes, stirring occasionally. Strain the contents through a sieve into another saucepan, pressing down on the solids and scraping the underside of the sieve, then cover and set aside until you're ready to serve.

To serve, slice the pork about ¹/3-inch thick and put on warm plates with the prunes; pour the gravy on the meat or pass separately.

Note: If you plan to eat this on a Saturday night, I suggest you make the marinade on the Thursday night, then put the pork in the marinade on Friday morning. On Saturday you can take the pork out, sear it, and refrigerate until

it's ready to be roasted with the prunes later.

BUTTERED BRUSSELS SPROUTS
Serves 8

This is so easy and might make a Brussels sprouts lover out of a Brussels sprouts hater—of which I know there are a few.

If you have any sprouts left over and by a miracle of luck have a little bowl of cold mashed potatoes lying around, you can make BUBBLE AND SQUEAK—a pillar (along with Spotted Dick, Clap Trap, and Cock-A-Leekie soup) of the British Empire. In a heavy pan set over high heat, melt a little bacon fat and add the mash and Brussels sprouts. Fry them together for ten to fifteen minutes, until they're well browned and even blackened in a few spots. Serve very hot with a crisply fried egg on top and lots of freshly ground black pepper . . . a guaranteed cure for being homesick for England—or it might make it worse.

2 ¹/2   pounds Brussels sprouts, trimmed and peeled

    2   tablespoons unsalted butter, including butter for the casserole

    2   teaspoons kosher salt

¹/2   teaspoon freshly ground black pepper

With a small sharp knife, cut each Brussels sprout into ¹/16-inch-thick slices. Bring a large saucepan of water to the boil, salt it well, and tip in the sliced Brussels sprouts. When the water comes back to a boil, set a timer and cook the sprouts for about 3 minutes; they should be just al dente.

Drain, and run under cold water to stop the cooking, then pat dry. Put the sprouts in a well-buttered casserole, dot with the remaining butter, cover with the lid (or aluminum foil), and set aside until you need them.

When you're ready, reheat in the lower third of a preheated 350°F oven for 30 minutes, or until very hot, then remove the lid, or foil and toss with the salt and black pepper just before serving.

POLENTA WITH FRESH SAGE
Serves 8 to 10

- 1/2 cup heavy cream
- 1 tablespoon kosher salt
- 1 teaspoon freshly ground black pepper
- 1 1/2 cups instant polenta (half a 500-gram packet)
- 1 bunch fresh sage

In a medium saucepan, bring 5 cups of water to a boil. Then, off the heat, add the cream, salt, and pepper. Sprinkle in the polenta, stirring constantly with a whisk. Put back over the heat and stir with the whisk until the polenta is thick, about 3 minutes.

Scrape around the pan with a rubber spatula to clean up the edges and cover with plastic wrap, pressed down onto the surface. For convenience, the polenta can be held for 1 hour by setting it over gently simmering water with a folded kitchen towel laying on top of the plastic wrap, to contain the heat

Just before serving, add about 1/2 cup of boiling water and whisk through vigorously to smooth. Then when the polenta is on the plate, scatter with fresh sage.

COFFEE CRÈME CARAMEL
Serves 8 to 10

THE CARAMEL

- 1 cup sugar

Put a 9-inch cake pan on a half sheet pan, and set aside. To make the caramel, put an 8-inch nonstick frying pan over medium-low heat; add the sugar in an even layer and stay nearby to keep an eye on it. If it starts darkly bubbling from under the sugar, turn the heat down and shake the pan, but don't stir. In 10 minutes, most of the sugar should have melted and caramelized. Stir to incorporate the surface sugar and mash any sugar lumps into the caramel with the back of a wooden spoon. Stir until the caramel is totally smooth and a dark golden brown, about another 2 minutes. Pour the caramel into the cake pan, and (wearing oven gloves) quickly tip the hot caramel around to coat the base and up the sides a little. Leave the container on a level surface for 2 minutes to let the caramel harden, then set aside while you make the coffee crème.

Position a rack in the lower third of the oven and preheat to 300°F.

THE COFFEE CRÈME

- 10 tablespoons sugar
- 4 tablespoons Medaglia d'Oro espresso coffee powder
- 4 cups whole milk
- 8 extra-large eggs
- 2 teaspoons pure vanilla extract

To make the coffee crème, mix the sugar and espresso powder in a medium saucepan, add the milk, and warm over medium heat until bubbles start forming around the edge.

Whisk the eggs and vanilla well in a medium bowl, then pour in about a cup of the hot milk mixture to raise the temperature, and whisk again. Add the rest of the hot milk and whisk to incorporate. Strain through a fine-mesh sieve into the caramel-lined pan and pour 1/2 inch of hot water into the sheet pan. Cover with a double sheet of aluminum foil just resting on top to stop a heavy skin forming and carefully put into the oven. After 1 1/4 hours, remove the foil and tap the side of the baking dish gently, watching the middle of the custard. You'll be able to see if the center is still actually liquid or if it has just jelled and kind of

shivers in the center. It should be nowhere near solid. Remove from the oven and set aside to cool, then leave it covered in the fridge at least overnight, or preferably for 2 nights. If you can make this crème caramel 48 hours ahead, the advantage is that all the caramel will have melted on the base instead of only half and you'll have more caramel to serve with the custard. When you come to turn it out, run a nonserrated knife ONCE around the edge, pressing against the side of the container. Place a plate with a rim or a slight depression (to hold the liquid caramel) on top of the custard and flip the whole thing over quickly and boldly, then slowly lift off the pan.

Return to the fridge until serving time; spoon a little caramel on top and serve at the table with Walnut Shortbread (recipe follows).

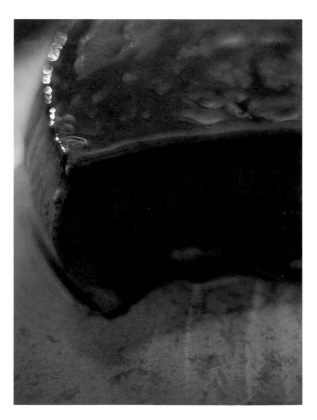

WALNUT SHORTBREAD
Makes 32 small shortbreads

If you don't cook a lot and have made this winter menu, I'm almost inclined to suggest you buy whatever cookies you like to go with dessert because *you're probably pounding on the kitchen door begging to be released.* But these cookies are so crisp, crumbly, and rich they're worth making at some point and are a perfect companion to the crème caramel, so you decide.

1 cup walnuts

1 1/2 cups Heckers or King Arthur all-purpose flour

1/4 cup granulated sugar

1/4 cup packed dark brown sugar

16 tablespoons (2 sticks) cold unsalted butter, cut into 1/2-inch cubes

1 teaspoon kosher salt

Position a rack in the upper third of the oven and preheat to 350°F.

Put all the ingredients in the bowl of a food processor in the order listed and blend for 8 to 10 seconds. Dump out onto a work surface and gather the crumbs into a heap. Starting at the back, push a section of the crumbs down and away with the heel of your hand to blend them together, working through the whole heap once or twice, but no more. You'll see how fast the mixture comes together—this method, called "pushing off," promotes the crumbly texture with a good bite that gives a great shortbread its distinctive character. Divide the dough into 4 equal pieces and roll each one out to a 4 1/2-inch circle. With a sharp knife cut each circle into 8 wedge-shaped pieces and press a walnut quarter firmly onto each one. Transfer to an unlined, sheet pan and bake for 13 to 15 minutes, or until the shortbreads are a dark golden brown.

These cookies keep really well in an airtight container, but I usually put them all out on the table and they disappear by the end of the meal. OR I wrap them for friends to take home because it's impossible for me to resist them first thing in the morning when I'm standing with a steaming cup of coffee . . . so, like Elvis, they have to leave the building.

CONVERSION CHARTS

WEIGHT EQUIVALENTS

The metric weights given in this chart are not exact equivalents, but have been rounded up or down slightly to make measuring easier.

VOLUME EQUIVALENTS

These are not exact equivalents for American cups and spoons, but have been rounded up or down slightly to make measuring easier.

OVEN TEMPERATURE EQUIVALENTS

Avoirdupois	Metric
1/4 oz	7 g
1/2 oz	15 g
1 oz	30 g
2 oz	60 g
3 oz	90 g
4 oz	115 g
5 oz	150 g
6 oz	175 g
7 oz	200 g
8 oz (1/2 lb)	225 g
9 oz	250 g
10 oz	300 g
11 oz	325 g
12 oz	350 g
13 oz	375 g
14 oz	400 g
15 oz	425 g
16 oz (1 lb)	450 g
11/2 lb	750 g
2 lb	900 g
21/4 lb	1 kg
3 lb	1.4 kg
4 lb	1.8 kg

American	Metric	Imperial
1/4 t	1.2 ml	
1/2 t	2.5 ml	
1 t	5.0 ml	
1/2 T (1.5 t)	7.5 ml	
1 T (3 t)	15 ml	
1/4 cup (4 T)	60 ml	2 fl oz
1/3 cup (5 T)	75 ml	21/2 fl oz
1/2 cup (8 T)	125 ml	4 fl oz
2/3 cup (10 T)	150 ml	5 fl oz
3/4 cup (12 T)	175 ml	6 fl oz
1 cup (16 T)	250 ml	8 fl oz
11/4 cups	300 ml	10 fl oz (1/2 pt)
11/2 cups	350 ml	12 fl oz
2 cups (1 pint)	500 ml	16 fl oz
21/2 cups	625 ml	20 fl oz (1 pint)
1 quart	1 liter	32 fl oz

Oven Mark	F	C	Gas
Very cool	250	130	1/2
	275	140	1
Cool	300	150	2
Warm	325	170	3
Moderate	350	180	4
Moderately hot	375	190	5
	400	200	6
Hot	425	220	7
	450	230	8
Very hot	475	250	9

STUFF

Ancho chili powder **6**
Aged sherry vinegar
    (Miguel & Valentino) **13**
Analon nonstick 12" round griddle **7**
Analon titanium 12" open stir fry **7**
Bacon (cob-smoked breakfast bacon) **5**
Candles **16**
Cardamom seeds **6**
Chipotle chili powder **3**
Chorizo (Palacios chorizo, hot) **13**
Chutneys: Delta Road, Hot Plum, Peach **1**
Coatrack **17**
Cocoa Barry, Extra Brute **11**
Crystallized roses **12**
Crystallized violets **12**
Cumberland sausages **8**
Dijon mustard (Amora) **3**
Dijon mustard (Maille) **3, 6, 15**
Dragées **9**
Fleur de Sel (French sea salt) **3, 6, 15**
Fruit purees: passion fruit and many
    others **10**
Ham (bone-in dinner ham,
    6 to 7 pounds) **5**
Herbes de Provence **3**
Jams: Apricot, Gingered Pear,
    Raspycran, Strawberry Rhubarb **1**
Maldon salt **3, 8**
Marcona almonds **13**
Medjool dates, extra-fancy **6**
Mini muffin tins (GourmetWare or
    Betty Crocker) **9**
Olive oil (Olio Santo extra virgin) **15**
Panko breadcrumbs **3**
Pickled ginger **3, 6**
Rose water (Lebanese) **3, 6, 9**
Sharpening stone (Japanese
    waterstone, ideally the Small
    Cerax Combination Stone) **4**
Silpat nonstick liners **9, 15**
Smoked paprika, sweet and hot **3**
Stilton cheese **8**
Vanilla beans **3, 6, 9**
Vincotto **2**
White Lily All-Purpose Flour **14**

ADDRESSES

1 Beth's Farm Kitchen
   P.O. Box 113
   Stuyvesant Falls, NY 12174
   (800) 331-JAMS
   www.bethsfarmkitchen.com

2 Di Palo Specialty Food
   200 Grand Street
   New York, NY 10013
   (212) 226-1033

3 EthnicGrocer.com
   www.ethnicgrocer.com
   (312) 373-1777

4 Fine Tools
   www.fine-tools.com

5 Harrington's of Vermont
   210 East Main Street
   Richmond, VT 05477
   (802) 434-4444
   www.harringtonham.com

6 Kalustyans
   123 Lexington Avenue
   New York, NY 10016
   P (212) 685-3451
     (800) 352-3451
   F (212) 683-8458
   www.kalustyans.com

7 Macy's
   www.macys.com
   Retail stores

8 Myers of Keswick
   634 Hudson Street
   New York, NY 10014
   P (212) 691-4194
   F (212) 691-7423

9 New York Cake and Baking
   Supplies
   56 West 22nd Street
   New York, NY 10010
   P (212) 675-CAKE
     (800) 942-2539
   F (212) 675-7099

10 Qzina Specialty Foods, Inc.
   P (800) 532-5269
   www.qzina.com
   Phone orders only

11 Surfas Restaurant and Supply
   8825 National Blvd.
   Culver City, CA 90232
   (310) 559-4770
   www.surfasonline.com

12 Sweet Celebrations
   (800) 328-6722

13 La Tienda
   (888) 472-1022
   www.tienda.com

14 White Lily Foods Company
   218 East Depot Street
   Knoxville, TN 37917
   (800) 264-5459
   www.whitelily.com

15 Williams-Sonoma
   (877) 812-6235
   www.williams-sonoma.com

16 Scented candles:

   Er'go Candles
   www.ergocandles.com
   "Scarborough Aire"

   Mistral
   www.nordstroms.com
   "Verveine"

   Votivo
   www.illumecandles.com
   "Red Currant"
   "Sea Island Grapefruit"

17 Hold Everything
   www.holdeverything.com

Project editor: Sandra Gilbert
Production director: Kim Tyner

Published in 2004 by
Stewart, Tabori & Chang
A Company of La Martinière Groupe
115 West 18th Street New York, NY 10011

Canadian Distribution:
Canadian Manda Group
One Atlantic Avenue, Suite 105 Toronto, Ontario M6K 3E7 Canada

Library of Congress Cataloging-in-Publication Data
Bass, Serena.
Serena, food and stories : feeding friends every hour of the day / Serena Bass;
photography by David Loftus and Andra Nelki; illustrations by David Croland.-- 1st ed.
p. cm.
Includes index.
ISBN 1-58479-347-3 (hardcover)
1. Entertaining. 2. Cookery, International. 3. Menus. I. Title.
TX731.B362 2004
642'.4--dc22

Designed by Sam Shahid and Co.
The text of this book was composed in Futura and Adobe Garamond.

Printed in Singapore

10 9 8 7 6 5 4 3 2 1
First Printing

Stewart, Tabori & Chang is a subsidiary of

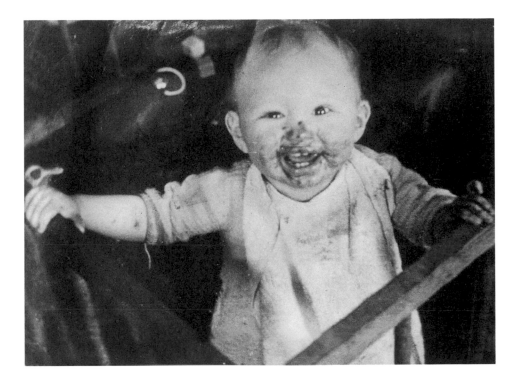

Brown